On the
WINGS
of the
CONDOR

BILL TOONE

Fellow of the Royal Geographical Society

CCS
PUBLICATIONS

On the Wings of the Condor
ISBN: 978-1-7331301-1-0
onthewingsofthecondor.com
Published by: CCS Publications

Editorial services by Misti Moyer

Cover design by: Linn Splane and Marisa Jackson
Interior design by Monica Thomas for TLC Book Design, *TLCBookDesign.com*

Cover imagery Monach butterfly, thawats, DepositPhotos.com,
Egg and feather by Sunni Black

Printed in the United States of America

Table of Contents

FOREWORD

Evolutionary biology is the study of adaptation, change, and progress in the unconscious pursuit of survival. A species may start primitive and through exposure and chance become a better creature, capable of living and thriving in a changing environment and, if lucky, improving the prospects of itself, its progeny, and even its species.

This is the story of the evolution of my good friend Bill Toone. From catcher-of-lizards to conservation visionary. A man who has had the great fortune—and adept perspective—to experience and learn from a life spent in work around our world and focused on conservation projects both effective and, in some cases, misguided.

I hope you will follow and derive some lesson from Bill's fascinating journey, and that you will, at some level, employ his call to support the conservation of our natural world in any way you can. We owe it to all those grandchildren and great-grandchildren, who need to catch lizards and observe the great wildebeest migration in our natural world. Thanks, Bill, for providing example and incentive in pursuit of survival.

~*TOM HANSCOM*
Public Relations Manager, Zoological Society of San Diego (retired)
Chairman emeritus for ECOLIFE Conservation

Chapter 1

THINGS THAT BITE *in the* NIGHT

"Men fear death as children fear to go in the dark…"
~SIR FRANCIS BACON

Everyone was speaking rapidly in Malagasy, but none of the chatter meant anything to me. Desperate to understand what was happening, I kept asking my translator, Tiana, to tell me what they were saying, but in the fear and confusion, she was silent. I knew I had to understand what was happening. I barked, "Tiana! You have to talk to me! You have to tell me what they are saying!"

She struggled to compose herself. Finally, through big wet tears, she mumbled quietly, "They are saying you are going to die."

I was nearing the end of a long visit to the tiny village of Antanambao in the remote forests of Madagascar. Each afternoon, the forest became impossibly hot just before dusk. Everyone in the village would simply lie down wherever they were and wait for it to pass. My wife Sunni and I were more cautious and would plan our day so that we could always retreat to our tents to try and nap until the evening took the edge off the heat.

Today, despite all my precautions, I was sick and days away from any sort of help. A vicious flu caused me to hurt every time I moved. I had dreaded this moment all day—the fever and chills combined with the smothering heat were not something I was looking forward to. To Sunni and me, our tents were always our safe place. They were nearly airtight, carefully designed and sealed to ward off everything from drenching rains to parasitic flies and malaria-ridden mosquitoes. The tent and its floor were one piece, everything from the ground up a very fine gnat-proof net. The floor was thin and water-resistant. Then, a rainfly covered the whole tent. We each crawled into our separate tents (it was too hot to share a tent) and zipped them closed. I filled the tiny gaps where the tent zippers met with twisted bits of toilet paper. My water was placed where I could find it and, next to the water, my flashlight, as it would soon be pitch black. Once I was organized and safe, I could settle in and try to rest.

I quickly realized that sealing myself into a hot tent was going to make a bad situation much worse. As soon as I settled down, another round of fever came, and the sweat poured from me. It dripped from my face and soaked my clothes. The tent was keeping the hot and cloyingly wet air inside. I felt like I was suffocating. Finally, I couldn't go another miserable moment without a lungful of the marginally fresher outside air, so I tugged at the tent zipper and made an opening of about eight inches. I pressed my mouth to the opening, took a deep breath of air from outside and finally drifted into a light restless sleep.

In doing this, I had broken my cardinal rule of remote tropical camping. The barrier between me and the outside world had a hole in it, and now, in that hazy place between wakefulness and sleep, I felt the faintest tickle on my chin. It had gotten dark, the kind of darkness that only the dense shelter of a rainforest could create. I knew this tickle was a mosquito, and I was glad I felt it before its little proboscis penetrated my skin and loaded me up with malarial plasmodium. Instinctively, I slapped at the tickle and knew instantly that I was wrong about it being a mosquito. It was large and hard, and the moment I slapped it, there was an instant and excruciatingly painful retaliation. The bite was like a dagger, and I knew instantly that it was poisonous. I could feel the heat radiate out from the bite to my chin and my cheek. The unexpected pain in the darkness terrified me, and in an out-of-body sort of way, I heard a truly blood-curdling scream. It was me. I sat up and desperately patted the floor in vain, searching for my flashlight. I was panicked by the bite and my inability to see what had bitten me. As I searched, I felt whatever had bitten me run up my arm and then down the back of my shirt. I panicked. I was already sick, incredibly hot, and had been bitten by a venomous unknown, which was now in my shirt. I was soaking with sweat and wiping at my dripping face in the dark. At this moment, I didn't know if it was drops of sweat or blood.

It is important to know that *no one* screamed in Antanambao. I had treated kids who had nearly chopped a finger off with a machete, not make a peep while I fussed with their wounds. Stoic was an understatement in this rugged community of forest-dwelling people. The reaction to my uncharacteristic outburst was instantaneous. It woke Sunni in her tent as well as most of the rest of the tiny community where we were camped. The sharp white beam of Sunni's flashlight sliced through the darkness as men from the village unzipped the door of my tent and dragged me out onto the ground. I could see Sunni's frightened face in the reflected light of the flashlight. I grabbed my shirt and whatever was in there and twisted it up in an effort to avoid another bite. While the men of the village worked on removing my shirt, I repeatedly snapped desperately at Tiana: "Am I bleeding?" and "What are they saying?"

There was so much liquid pouring off my face and so little light that I couldn't tell if it was sweat or blood. My terror was contagious, and Tiana stood there mute and crying. Petrified largely by my fear, Sunni and Tiana could only watch as my shirt was peeled off.

As the twisted knot I had made in the back of my shirt was finally opened, an eight-inch tropical centipede launched itself back into the darkness of the tent. Named for the pairs of feet on each of its dozens of body segments, this centipede was large enough to eat small lizards, birds, and even small mammals. Its mouth was armed with two large hypodermic fangs to inject poison and subdue its prey. At least one of those fangs had found my chin. Once they knew what it was, everything happened in a violent flurry. Two men left the tiny village at a dead run, presumably to find help, while two others pursued the centipede back into my tent. The chief's wife, Marie Ange, took hold of my face and, with her strong hands and garden-toughened nails, dug into my chin and pinched away the flesh at the site of the bite. The fresh, deep wound was then drenched with a locally made kerosene, a standard but painful treatment.

Chapter 2

CHICKENS SET MY PATH *for the* FUTURE

"I consider it the best part of an education to have been
born and brought up in the country."

-AMOS BRONSON ALCOTT

I have always had an inexplicable passion for all things natural. As a child, I wanted to nourish and care for every creature I could find. There were boys who loved snakes because it would bring them attention, and they could chase girls with them. Not me, I just really loved snakes, and lizards, and bugs, and spiders, and possums, and skunks—they were my friends. Growing up where

11

we were the only house around probably had some influence on my choice of friends. While my parents did not understand my excitement for nature, they were supportive of my passion, which didn't hurt. But still, it was a little boy's passion. By that, I mean that it was undirected and, all too often, misdirected. I had a desire to catch what I saw and loved, which was not always in the best interest of the creature I had discovered. Ultimately, this youthful exuberance launched me into the largest single species recovery program in the United States. It ratified, in so many ways, the things I had believed in as a child and that were taught in school. Unfortunately, many years later, a little boy in Madagascar would destroy all of this, and two conservation programs I was leading would collapse in failure. This is a story of this love for nature coming of age over more than fifty years of exploring all that the wild world had to offer and how, figuratively speaking, I went from picking flowers to appreciating flowers and finally to planting them.

I grew up in the 1950s and 1960s in Poway, part of rural San Diego County. Back then, it was a small, mostly poor country town. Despite its reputation, Southern California was (and still is) a surprisingly conservative community. I came of age on the tail end of the Vietnam War protests and truly classic rock-n-roll music. My parents objected to both of these. People hated John Lennon for claiming that the Beatles were "more popular than Jesus" and were troubled when Martin Luther King, Jr., shared his dream and led the March on Washington. The gossip machine in our small town went wild when the minister at our community church started growing his hair long—a transgression that ended my formal religious education because my father, a one-time want-to-be preacher, pulled us from church and started holding Sunday school in our living room. Eventually, Dad gave up on teaching the Bible, and I gave up on believing in what was in it. In the end, though, I was raised with solid principles of respect for everyone and everything, honesty, and hard work.

Summers were hot, with the evenings tempered by breezes from the Pacific Ocean that lay twenty miles to the west. In the fall, hot winds, called Santa Anas, would blow off the desert from the east and blow tumbleweeds across the fields. These winds would often fan wildfires in the dry chaparral, and when that happened, my friends and I would grab a shovel and hoe and help the local fire department stomp them out. Things have changed. The fires are bigger, and we are smart to flee as legions of professional firefighters put their lives on the line.

Our home was a simple stucco rectangular affair located in the middle of pretty much nowhere. As it turned out, "the middle of nowhere" would pretty much describe where I was for most of the rest of my life. It was the only house at the end of a sidewalk-free road in a giant stretch of sagebrush, rattlesnakes, and boulders. The soil, such as it was, we called the Poway conglomerate. It was made up of large pads of decomposing granite, clay, and rocks. My parents had fled family and work issues in New Jersey, my dad a Protestant and my mom a Catholic. It was here in the tiny town of Poway that they had decided to start a new life, secure in the belief that nobody was likely to follow them.

My dad was tall and lanky and always kept his hair in a pretty tight buzz cut. After he retired, he made a feeble and, thankfully, brief attempt at a mustache, but that was about it for flash and style. He was a man of faith, a conservative, and a juvenile probation officer who took his work seriously and deeply to heart. It hurt him in ways we could never know, but we knew to leave him alone when he came home from work. He needed an hour to become clean again. He would get a beer and disappear into the family room, where he would listen to classical music before joining the family in the kitchen. I caught him once crying as he listened. For a man who was tough and hardened to the point of being distant, this was a contrast I couldn't reconcile as a child. Imbued with traditional values, Dad went to work every morning, in a coat and tie, at 7:30 a.m. sharp, while Mom stayed home and took care of the family and most of our day-to-day issues. In contrast to Dad, Mom was short, prone to a little extra weight, and proud to be Italian. She was the warmth in the family. Dad could teach me to drive nails and fix leaky pipes, but it was Mom who you went to when you needed a hug or to learn about life and love.

While Dad too often seemed emotionally distant, his passion for his family and creating a good life for us was never questioned. I can remember quite clearly my dad's first attempt at creating a lawn outside the back door. He pounded away at the rocks and clay with a pick and shovel. He brought in topsoil, made a little wood lath border, and planted a dichondra lawn. Dichondra is not a blade grass but a very delicate ground cover. It does not handle much traffic or wear, and you never mow it. It loves and needs water all the time. It was really lush and beautiful but very fragile. As I look back, this was probably not a great choice in a dry desert environment, and an even worse decision for a family with four young kids and a dog. Watering the lawn was practically a full-time job, and the introduction of that much water in the middle of hot dry sage attracted all sorts of living things. It was here along the dichondra lawn that I got my first lessons in biology.

First came the concept of edge, that place where one habitat type merges with another. These areas tend to be very fertile for a diversity of living things, and for me, that first biological edge was where the wet dichondra met the dry cement patio. Here, where water pooled and drained from the patio, the lawn grew denser and taller and attracted all sorts of pill bugs, worms, and more. I would start at one end of the patio and pull the lawn away from the concrete and work my way down the patio looking for bugs, unknowingly leaving a trail of destruction in the delicate dichondra as I went.

Seeing bugs work their way through moist humus and feeding on decaying vegetation was great, but the next lesson was a little more graphic. As I worked my way down the edge, watching for movement, I found myself staring into an unusual little face. Mostly, it was unusual because it had four eyes, one pair set right behind the other. Too many for a lizard and not enough for a spider. This creature stared up at me with its four glassy, bulging eyes. It took a moment for the image to distill. I was, in fact, looking at a small snake swallowing a small frog, hind end first. The frog's head, from the eyes forward, was all that was sticking out of the snake's mouth. This allowed both of them to stare eerily up at me. There it was: eat or be eaten. This grittiness of nature up close and personal never repelled me. Instead, it intrigued me and made me more curious.

For years, Dad worked in the sun and harvested the rocks from the dry soil in an attempt to create a beautiful place for our family to enjoy. To dispose of the rocks, he surrounded our property with neatly built rock walls. I, in turn, spent a lot of time following behind him, tearing the walls down in search of lizards and snakes. I used to think of my dad as being a terrible grump. Today, as I care for my own yard, I am amazed at his patience.

First lesson in field biology: learning how to hold a snake so I would not be bitten and the snake would be unharmed.

To my parents' credit, rather than try to divert or retrain a curious and destructive child, they chose to foster my interests. Their first attempt to bring my love of bugs, lizards, and snakes to a higher level occurred when I was six years old. They took the family to the San Diego Zoo. Mom, Dad, and the four of us kids had barely made it through the gate when my attention was captured by a banty hen and her large collection of cute, fluffy, newly hatched chicks. The mother hen, puffed up and protective in her broodiness, hovered over the chicks clucking reassurances to them while I hovered over her. These chickens would forever change the course of my life. My siblings grew tired of the chickens, eager to see more of the zoo. After all, there were apes that we could see as caricatures of ourselves, lions to impress us, snakes to frighten us, but none of that was going to work for me. In fact, I was so reluctant to leave the avian family that I spoiled the day's experience for the rest of my family. Later that day, I got time alone in my room. I don't remember now if that time alone was a punishment for ruining the day or another way Mom and Dad were mentoring my interests. Regardless of the cause, I used the time to sit at my desk and draft a short note to the zoo's curator of birds, expressing my complete fascination with his chickens.

Within days of sending that note, K.C. Lint, the San Diego Zoo's curator of birds and my soon-to-be hero, called my parents and told them that if they would bring me to the zoo, he would give me some chickens. And so, my love affair with birds and nature, in general, began to take a serious form. K.C. met my family at the front of the zoo and gave me a cardboard box with four half-grown chickens in it. The rooster, along with his three hens, became my door into the world of birds, and because of that, K.C. and I would meet again.

They were a small breed known as the silkie bantam. While one should never speak badly of a gift, the fact was that they were actually a bit of a disappointment. The banty chickens I had fallen in love with were the Indian red jungle fowl, a sleek, colorful, wild bird from the forests of India, Indochina, and China. But the domesticated silkie bantams were more like the fluffy white poodles of the bird world. Their feathers lacked barbules and, therefore, were more fluffy down than actual feathers. As a result, they would never fly, and they looked goofy. Even then, I knew they would never survive in a jungle, and that was a bit of an embarrassment. I always figured that was why the zoo gave them away.

I swallowed my disappointment, though, and read up on silkie bantams. Today, I recognize another sign of good parenting by my father. In the 1960s, there was no Google. You had to go to a library, use the card index, and then check out a book. I was too young to do that, but somehow the information on my chickens kept showing up. My dad's lunch hour was religiously devoted to supporting the curiosity of his children. Through the books my dad brought home, I learned that, unlike the wild red jungle fowl, these were fully domesticated chickens with an amazing reputation for being good mothers. I played on that characteristic and must have made the chickens crazy. I collected wild duck and quail eggs and put them under the unsuspecting hens in the place of their own eggs. Baffled, they raised unusual babies, while my supportive parents built aviaries and supported my passion. By the time I was eight years old, I had a small collection of birds and was certain my career path had been set. I was going to be the curator of birds at the San Diego Zoo.

Without any real concept of a resume, I wrote a letter that described my extensive experience. In my mind, I had already done an animal transaction with the zoo and successfully received four chickens. I had proven I could collect wild animals by snatching eggs from the nearby duck pond and could raise birds, as proven by my ever-growing collection. At eight years old, I could not imagine anyone else with the diversity of skills I was offering to the zoo. I put the letter into an envelope that I carefully stamped and put it in the mailbox at the end of the driveway. We didn't get a lot of mail, so I was sure to put the red flag all the way up so the postman would know there was a letter to go out. I sent the letter to Dr. Charles Schroeder, the zoo's executive director. Somehow, deep inside, I knew that K.C. Lint would not give up his job willingly, so it was best to go straight to his boss with my appeal.

Every day, I waited for a phone call or letter, and every day seemed interminably long. No call ever came, but finally, there was a small letter in the box. I can still picture every detail of the letter I received in return from the director—it had the old zoo logo atop a 5.5″ by 8.5″ piece of paper. In a somewhat lengthy first paragraph, Dr. Schroeder listed a litany of reasons why I couldn't have the job. Something about my age, a driver's license, and a high school diploma—a lot of hollow excuses, in my opinion. In the last paragraph, he made a strategic error.

The year was 1963, and Dr. Schroeder was already dreaming of a North County campus, which would be known as the San Diego Wild Animal Park and later as the San Diego Zoo Safari Park. He wrote in the last paragraph that he hoped the park would open about the same time I turned sixteen and that if I was still interested in animals and wanted to work for the zoo, he would give me a job. I suppose, like many of us, we mostly see and hear what we want. I didn't really absorb anything about not being able to work there; instead, I read, "When you turn sixteen, I will give you a job." The letter was carefully folded, put back into its envelope, and stuffed into the top right-hand drawer of my dresser under my socks. This was great. I was only eight years old, and my life was all laid out for me.

I maintained my interests, and right after my sixteenth birthday, I exercised my brand-new driver's license by driving to the zoo to keep an appointment with the director. I arrived at his office, the eight-year-old letter in my hand, and informed him I was there for my job. Dr. Schroeder's dream park was not yet open to the public, but he was a man of his word. So it came to be that I started working for the Zoological Society of San Diego. Although I was hoping to be the new curator of birds, or maybe a bird keeper, it did not turn out exactly that way. I was given a job picking up trash at a yet-to-be-opened park.

This lesson of perseverance was not lost on me. It never occurred to me that this was not the job I wanted. I was now working for the zoo. It was a first step towards the goal and, therefore, a success. No matter how small the steps, I never lost sight of where they might take me.

Chapter 3

WORKING
at the
WILD ANIMAL PARK

"The way to get started is to quit talking and begin doing."
~WALT DISNEY

I was given a job at Dr. Schroeder's dream come true, the San Diego Wild Animal Park (SDWAP), now called the San Diego Zoo's Safari Park. At the time of its opening, it was an 1,800-acre park with large open enclosures where herds of mixed species could roam freely. One enclosure at the park could hold the entire San Diego Zoo and its parking lot. In 1972, this represented a new and revolutionary vision for a zoo.

Because the park was not yet open to the public and seeing as my job was to pick up trash dropped by visitors who were not there, I found myself with time on my hands. I happily filled my free time reading the new signs being installed on animal exhibits and watching the animal keepers and amazing wild creatures adapt to their new surroundings. I saw this job as an exciting entry into a world of animals much bigger and more exciting than those found in either our dichondra lawn, the scrub of rural Poway, or my chicken coop.

With a job, a fancy new uniform, and a fat ring of keys that mostly opened the rooms where the mops and toilet paper were kept, my self-confidence grew. I was a bit of a nerd and always a little out of place in school. I was an October baby and, therefore, almost a year younger than most of my classmates. That issue was exacerbated by the fact that physically, I was a late bloomer. Suffice it to say, I was never picked for any teams while in school, but at the Wild Animal Park, I was surrounded by people of similar interests. It was refreshing and inspiring. I felt I had finally found a team where I could fit in.

I was crazy about animals. As my comfort grew, I became more outgoing and made an effort to meet everyone at the park. I acted like an animal keeper at every possible opportunity; I tried to look like one, talk like one, and most of all, to know the animals like one. But I never let my dreams affect my more immediate job. I was armed during the day with a woven nylon bag on a handle and a pair of trash tongs to pick up bits of debris mindlessly dropped by visitors. I worked on getting insanely proficient with the trash picker; besides napkins, paper cups, and bags, I could grab tiny bits of paper, matchsticks, and cigarette butts. To me, being proficient also meant being fast. I simply wanted to be the best. There were still a lot of smokers back then, and I was like a vulture lurking nearby, waiting for them to drop their cigarette butts. Too often, my speed led me to grab hot butts, which too frequently caught my trash bag on fire. I would not be stopped though, so I simply refined my technique to include squashing the hot end of the cigarette as I grabbed it.

I took any shift and any job they gave me. I mopped floors until 1:30 in the morning with a cranky old Italian janitor named Lou Lavigne. Lou was tall and lean with a wrinkled, leathery face, perpetually sucking deeply on a cigarette. He was grumpy, outspoken, and a bit of a challenge to get along with. Everyone agreed that the lonely night shift was perfect for Lou. He could be tough and irascible, and only the new part-time help had to deal with it. He scared me, but I tried to get along with him, and I think in his own way, he really appreciated that. At sixteen, I had no idea that there was a right way to swing a mop, but Lou showed me that there was. Nothing was more rewarding than going through the thousands of square feet of the gift shop and looking back at a streak-free floor. Lou was proud of his work and taught me the same principles. I can still swing a mop with pride and efficiency.

Finally, I could go to parties with people I liked and who liked me. At my first employee party, still too young to legally drink, I was over-served red wine. I loved it and had fun. It felt great right up until that moment where I did not feel so great. It would be more than twenty years before I could drink red wine again. The following day, the alarm went off before dawn because I was scheduled for a 6:00 a.m. shift, but I was not up to it. I was nauseous, had a headache like I had never imagined, and the whole world was spinning. I called the park security and told them I was sick and would miss my shift. A few minutes later, the phone rang. It was my supervisor, a kind but hard-nosed ex-submariner named Don Carlson. Don blinked constantly, apparently a twitch that I was told was somehow associated with pressure issues encountered in his work on submarines. He informed me he had seen me the night before, and I needed to get my rear end to work. Painfully, and with the world still spinning, I made it to the employee entrance at the park. There was Mr. Carlson, waiting in an electric trash cart. He motioned me aboard, and we drove off in silence. He parked the cart behind the big hay barn out of everyone's sight and got out. He knew I couldn't work and said, "You just sit here. I'll come get you at the end of your shift."

I sat right there for four hours before he finally came striding back. Don looked right at me. "Bill, you applied for this job like an adult, and I gave you one. It is your responsibility to manage your life so that you can show up and meet your commitments." I was terrified, but he continued, "You can have fun with your friends, but never forget how your actions will impact your next steps." Hoping it would end, I nodded with a sincere look of understanding, but he wasn't finished. "I hope we never have to talk about this again." It had an enormous impact on me. This was my chance of a lifetime, and I was about to lose it. I apologized and promised that we would never have to talk about it again, and we didn't. He became a big supporter of mine and rehired me into his department countless times during my early years at the park. I learned a lot about always doing my best and leaving behind a good impression.

My feverish desire to be good at picking up trash and my willingness to do anything at any time opened the doors I had hoped for. I was given the opportunity to be a guide and tell guests about the animals while driving a monorail on a five-mile-long track. At the San Diego Zoo, the guides drove buses, but at the Wild Animal Park, we had these amazing, large two-car silent electric monorails—a mode of transportation that was well ahead of its time, especially for a zoo.

Of course, everything was about marketing, and it seemed important to have an exotic name for this state-of-the-art train system. In every way, the Wild Animal Park was Dr. Schroeder's baby, and he was always very proper and professional. Unfortunately, or maybe fortunately, he was out of town attending meetings while the zoo staff brainstormed a name for the train system. One frustrated staffer wrote down WGASA on a scrap of paper and slid it over to a colleague. It was assumed that this was a suggestion of a name for the monorail, and the exotic-sounding name caught on like wildfire. It turned out that WGASA was an acronym for how some staff were feeling about the naming process. "Who Gives a Shit Anyway" was really what they meant. So, without the adult supervision of Dr. Schroeder, the WGASA Bush Line was launched.

Rumors of the word's off-color meaning soon circulated. Charles Bieler, our fast-thinking development director, came up with a face-saving byline, telling everyone that it stood for "World's Greatest Animal Show Around." It was years later, when I was in management and Dr. Schroeder was sending me to Great Britain on the zoo's behalf, that he told me I would meet the duke of such-and-such and that while I was with the duke, it was likely that I would also meet the duchess of here-and-there. He smiled as he told me these two nobles were close and held up his hand horizontally with his index and third fingers crossed. "Close, like this." Then with a devilish smile, he added, "This is the duke on top," pointing to the finger crossed over the top of the other. I couldn't help but think that maybe the boss liked the name WGASA after all.

At seventeen years old, I was the youngest driver guide ever hired, and I relished it. The train rode on a concrete roadbed with a giant steel rail to guide it. The monorails were big and top-heavy, so low speeds on the curves were essential for everyone's safety. The trains were driven by nearly silent electric motors and relied on heavy-duty hydraulic brakes to handle the momentum of the huge car. In case of emergency, they were equipped with a deadman pedal and an overspeed brake. If you lifted your foot from the deadman, within seconds, the brakes would lock, and the train would go into a screeching, sliding, and sudden stop. The same thing would happen if you went too fast. When the train stopped like that, loaded with over a hundred parents and children innocently enjoying a holiday, it could cause a bit of panic when the brakes kicked in. Two huge train cars weighing a couple of tons would screech to an instant stop, pitching everyone forward out of their seats. Traumatic for everyone and embarrassing for the negligent driver. But accidents happened, and if they happened often enough, you learned how to cover for it. It turned out that where you fed lots of animals, you attracted thousands of squirrels and rabbits. On the rare occasion when I released the deadman or went too fast, I would quickly announce that we had just avoided hitting a bunny. Inevitably, our shaken guests would break out into applause. Just a tiny white fabrication, but effective. I did not realize at the time how valuable the skills of sharing a story would be, but I am forever grateful.

Finally, I landed a temporary job as a hospital keeper while the regular keeper was on vacation. I worked hard and earned my stripes. Shortly after that, I was hired as an attendant in the Animal Care Center (ACC). Though I was doing the work of a keeper, that was not my title, and here's why: zoos are pretty traditional, and in a conservative community like San Diego, the zoo was, and is, monumentally slow to change. As an example, Belle Benchley was a prominent name in the zoo world. In San Diego, she served as one of their finest executive directors from 1927 to 1953. For the early part of her career, she was deprived of that title because she was a woman and was instead called the zoo's executive secretary. In those years, it was probably not too unusual to withhold the rightful title, yet it was forward thinking for her to hold the job. Anyway, in the ACC, we cared for babies and sick or injured animals. The "keepers" were all women, and as a result, they were called attendants. I was the first male to work in the ACC, and like the amazing women I worked with, I too was called an attendant.

At the time, the ACC was split essentially into four sections: a paddock of goats and tame animals for families to interact with called the Petting Kraal; a section for baby or injured hoofstock (antelopes, gazelles, giraffes, rhinos, and more); a big, open kitchen; and a fourth section for the more sensitive and valuable babies like cheetahs, gorillas, and orangutans. Since I was young and inexperienced, any day shift I was on would generally be with the goats, maybe sometimes with the hoofstock. I made the best of it by keeping the animals protected from our guests (and vice versa) and, in our alone time, playing with the billy goats. Headbutting was a ritual for them, and our herd was mostly made up of small but feisty pygmy goats. Peter the billy goat defined feisty. He would spend much of the day chasing me around in pursuit of mock battles. Billy goats have a very stinky gland at the base of each horn, and by the end of the day, I had enough pungent odor on me that my mother would not allow me in the house after work. There was always a change of clothes in the garage when I got home. Through some strange process of habituation, I was mostly unaware of the odor.

Though I was fighting my way through school, I was young. Late-night hours left my days wide open. I could work until the wee hours and still get to school for classes. As it was, when I was still working on the cleaning crew, I had always been happy to come in on the night shift and mop floors until 1:30 in the morning. When I was finally offered a night shift taking care of sick and baby animals, it was like a dream come true! The night shift was different because it meant that I was there alone, and it was mine, all of it. The pesky goats were asleep, the public gone, the hoofstock fed, and the baby gorilla named Jim wanted to play.

The Wild Animal Park tried a lot of things to have a successful birth of a lowland gorilla. I clearly remember that the staff had a TV in the gorilla bedrooms and were showing them movies. Of course, I assumed they were "inspirational" sex videos, but apparently, I was misinformed. I do know they showed movies of mother gorillas caring for their babies, which seemed remarkably dull given the options and probably a bit confusing. I could not help but picture the gorilla scratching its head and thinking, "Okay, but how does the baby gorilla get here?"

Baby Jim was a western lowland gorilla born at the Wild Animal Park in 1973, and despite the instructional movies, he was largely ignored by his inexperienced mother, Dolly. He was taken from his mother to be raised by attendants and spent the first part of his life in the ACC alongside another great ape baby, an orangutan named Guy. The contrast between these two great apes were as amazing as the similarities that all of us great apes share. With the differences in human and chimpanzee DNA coding amounting to only about 1.2%, we are more similar to each other than we are different. Despite these genetic similarities, each of the great apes are unique but in the case of Jim the gorilla and Guy the orangutan, the contrast was like day and night. Orangutans are loners who live mostly solitary lives in the treetops, while gorillas are social animals who live in extended family groups and are much more comfortable spending most of their day on the ground. Like their wild peers, Guy the orangutan was more delicate and retiring. Jim, on the other hand, was rambunctious, outgoing, and decidedly social. Jim and I must have shared more DNA than usual because we hit it off immediately.

Though it was fun, it was not all sweetness and light; there were days when the feces flew. Both Jim and Guy wore diapers as babies, and that was a challenge. These two apes were far more physically advanced than human children of the same age. I know from experience that diapering these particular children can be more challenging than diapering a human. With humans, you can pin a pair of diapers on a baby, and neither our fingers nor our brains are developed enough to solve the puzzle offered by a safety pin. Safety pins were a mystery to Jim for all of about twenty seconds. After that, he would be diaperless and armed with two sharp pins, and all of this was bad.

We developed our own technique of folding the diaper in such a manner that we could run a rope through the diaper and around Jim's waist. Once tightly knotted, the rope would be shifted around until the knot was under a tight fold in the back. I know this sounds ridiculously easy to do, but Jim was about thirty pounds of sheer muscle at the time and not inclined to hold still. He could bite and grab you with equal effectiveness with his feet, his hands, or all of the

My time with Jim was a memorable gift in life. We were together only a short time, but he left a permanent mark deep in my soul.

above. In reality, if Jim was not willing to be diapered, he wouldn't be. To his credit, he wore diapers most of the time.

Once diapered, the hard part was done. Now it was playtime. There was a food preparation area that resembled the set-up for a huge buffet. During the day, it was bustling with keepers (the real ones, not "attendants" like me), chopping a range of things to make amazing culinary concoctions to fit the palates of our finicky international collection. Cases of apples, oranges, and bananas sat beside big tubs of writhing mealworms, chirping crickets, boxes of frozen baby mice, adult mice, rats, mackerel, chickens, and more. Next to the giant walk-in refrigerator was a long stainless steel food processing counter. Facing the public was a sloped area with a lip to hold food trays on display for the guests.

At night, this very busy place went quiet. Jim and I could raid the refrigerator and play on the counters. It became our routine to get Jim properly diapered, then place a big grey trash can at one end of the counter. We would go back to the other end, and I would grab Jim by his diaper and fling him down the slanted portion, where he would slide on the lip of the counter. With his hairy body and cotton diaper, he had very little resistance and would fly down the counter with squeals of enthusiasm and into the trash can. It was kind of like a flat roller coaster with a sudden drop and stop at the end. It was a great way to polish the counters. As soon as he landed in the trash can, he would grunt with pleasure, wearing a somewhat tortured-looking grin, and then he was out and ready to go again, over and over. Just before first light, when the real keepers came in, we would have to wrap it up. Jim knew it and hated that part. If I told him, "One more time and then we are done," he would fly down the counter, and then once in the trash can, he would go silent. Tucked tightly in the bottom, Jim would push against the sides with all his angry might and refuse to come out. More than once, keepers came in at first light to find my head in a trash can with the gorilla screaming like he had been stabbed with a safety pin.

One day, Jim was invited to be on *The Tonight Show* with Johnny Carson. Actually, it was Joan Embery, the zoo's goodwill ambassador, who was invited, but on this particular night, the plan was to bring a clouded leopard, a hooded cobra, and Jim. It would be an adventure that would go well into the night. Each of the selected animals needed a specialized keeper, and I would be Jim's.

So, on New Year's Day 1975, we piled into two giant zoo station wagons with Joan Embery and her husband Duane in the front seat, me in the back, and Jim, the clouded leopard, and the cobra all in their respective containers and off we went. While this might seem perfectly normal to us, it was not to Jim. He screamed continually, pitifully, and finally, angrily in his crate. The drive was easily two hours long, and only minutes into it, everyone's patience was wearing thin. Duane was trying to navigate a crowded freeway and finally asked if there was something I could do to silence the gorilla. Doing 65 mph on the freeway limited my options to only one: I could try letting him out of the crate.

We were all banking on the hope that all Jim needed was a little reassurance—that hug we all sometimes need when life gets a little wacky. I hung over the backseat and released the latches on Jim's crate. He burst out whimpering in a childlike way and launched himself firmly into my arms, where he held on for dear life. This was what we were hoping for. There was a certain beauty to being embraced by a small gorilla, his arms around my neck, legs around my chest, and all with a grip that suggested you meant everything to him. Though Jim was still an infant, his body was amazing. His broad, hairy back was muscular and rock hard. His chest was enviable, to say the least, and wide, every muscle clearly cut and tapering down to his narrow waist. It was like holding a spectacular man-child in my arms. At long last, there was relative silence in the car. I was calm, and most importantly, Jim, now securely in my arms, was calm, quiet, and under control. Everyone's blood pressure dropped ten to twenty points.

All of my short life had been about animals. Once I started working for the SDWAP, it evolved quickly, but I was slow to realize how different my life was from the way other people lived. Truth was, I did not appreciate how abnormal my life had become. For example, it hadn't really occurred to me how it might look to people in another car to see a teenager being hugged by a gorilla in a station wagon. Apparently, it looked odd. With valuable cargo, we were driving at or just below the speed limit so a car would shoot by us, and then brake lights would come on as it slowed to let us catch up so they could get another look. Jim made eye contact with the driver, and the game was on. From one side of the car to the other, Jim and I played with traffic all the way to the studios. It likely took hours before traffic on the highway was back to normal.

The excitement did not end there. Jim was truly a guest of honor, and we had our own personal dressing room with drinks, a bowl of fruit, and so much more. This was all laid out like an amazing display of consumables, most of which was not part of Jim's carefully regulated diet. It was my job to keep Jim on his diet, so all hell broke loose as he leapt out of my arms, diving for what must have looked like a heavenly buffet. We wrestled madly for bananas and apples, drinks and napkins, glasses and plates. All I could do was occasionally get ahold of his diaper or the food items he was clenching, either in his mouth, his feet, or his hands. Jim had the advantage, as he was unconcerned about much of anything other than getting what he wanted. In no time at all, the room looked like an angry gorilla's dressing room. Johnny had a tradition of saying hello to each guest just prior to the show, presumably to calm any angst that his guests might feel. With food and baskets scattered everywhere, me holding onto Jim's diaper, and my clothes and hair badly disheveled, there was a tap on the door, and Johnny's famous face peeked in. That was all. The door was shut quietly, and we were left alone.

Joan and I met backstage so I could transfer Jim from my arms to hers. Jim and I were long-time friends, but this was the first day he had seen Joan in a very long time. He was not sure that she was going to be his friend, or if he would be hers. We tried a number of tricks, but he wasn't willing to go into Joan's arms. I sat behind him, giving him his bottle, and Joan and I would try to trade places. It simply didn't work. Joan, pulling from years of animal experience, said, "Bill, why don't you sit Jim down and leave the room while I try to feed him? I will be the only one he will recognize, and he will look to me for comfort instead of you." I thought it was a brilliant lesson from a sage, so I put Jim on the floor with his bottle and quickly slipped out. Moments later, someone rushed out to get me. He had panicked in my absence and was running around backstage looking for me. Jim was short, and it was hard to recognize people based solely on their knees. He was running to the nearest leg, looking up for comfort, and when it wasn't there, he was inclined to give a nip and run to the next person. There was uncontrolled mayhem until I managed to get myself in front of Jim, cutting him off from his next potential victim. In my case, I got the nip in the leg before he looked up, but it was magic when he saw it was me. He leapt, crying into my arms. It became painfully clear that he was not going on stage held by Joan. In her own way, she made it equally clear that Jim would not go on stage held by me! Jim ended up in a hastily improvised crib/cage and went on stage behind bars. Once he met Johnny, Jim became fully charming. As he and Johnny played tug of war through the cage's mesh, you would have never imagined the chaos he had created behind the curtain only moments before.

The time had come when we were all behind the curtain of *The Tonight Show*. A snake hook and hooded cobra in the hands of Tom Schultz, the zoo's reptile curator; a gorilla in diapers (with a handler, me, who was barely out of them himself); and a half-grown leopard with another very young, very new keeper. Tom had more experience than the two of us combined, which turned out to be valuable. With the first blast of music from Doc Severinsen and *The Tonight Show* band, the clouded leopard bolted away from its keeper, hit the back curtain about four feet off the ground, and started climbing for lights and glory.

Tom knew instantly that without immediate action, we would have a leopard up in the overhead lights in a studio with a full audience and cameras rolling. He must have rolled through scenarios that all started with evacuation and went downhill from there in a matter of a nanosecond. With no concern for his own safety, he abandoned the cobra (still safely in a pillowcase at this point) and leapt at the leopard before it got out of reach. He was able to grab the leopard's hind feet and, with a swift jerk, loosen the leopard's grip on the curtain. The leopard was now airborne, with Tom holding on. As only a cat in the air can do, the leopard found its center of balance, twisted around, flipped, and landed on Tom's back. Tom fell to his right side with the leopard on top of him. Together, we quickly fought to get the leopard under control, but by the time we were done, Tom and his uniform were both pretty damaged. We patched his shirt together in the back and tried to daub away the blood welling up under the material. Tom would not present the cobra tonight. Hastily patched together, he helped to move a box full of sand onto the stage in front of the audience, where the cobra would be presented by his colleague Robin. Then he slipped away before the cameras came around, leaving the audience with no clue about what had happened behind the curtain. This experience left me filled with admiration for Tom and a firm appreciation for his professionalism and depth of experience. Truly a great animal handler, and on top of that, he knew that the show must go on!

Jim grew up to be a 350-pound beautiful adult silverback, but his life was cut short by cancer when he was only thirteen years old. He left his mark on my heart and some lasting memories that greatly influenced my future. Though it would be many years in between, gorillas would again be important in my life.

Chapter 4

MY INTEREST
in Sexual
REPRODUCTION
Leads to
COLLEGE

"The more that you read, the more things you will know.
The more that you learn, the more places you'll go."
—*DR. SEUSS*

While Jim and I got along like thieves, and I enjoyed helping raise cheetahs, Przewalski's horses, giraffes, rhinoceroses, and more, none of the animals piqued my scientific curiosity quite like Charlie and Susie. The zoo purchased these two Abyssinian ground hornbills from a dealer in Holland in 1953. They were valuable birds, and the zoo hoped they would reproduce and bring a few more much-needed dollars into the zoo's coffers. To everyone's disappointment, Charlie devoted himself only to the early portions of courtship—the defense of territory and the constant offering of tasty bits to Susie. This territorial defense generally included harsh attacks on keepers and zoo visitors, when possible, with powerful strikes from a formidable and pointy beak. The other early courtship behavior consisted of constantly offering dead things to Susie. This meant he spent most of his day carrying dead rats or day-old chickens around in his beak in an effort to get Susie's attention. As for making babies, it was perhaps as fortunate for the guests as it was a disappointment for the zoo that he did not add that to his repertoire of public or private behaviors.

K.C. Lint was still the curator of birds for the San Diego Zoo. As such, he needed to make a decision about Charlie and Susie. Shortly before I started at the park, Mr. Lint had Charlie and Susie moved from their home of twenty years at the San Diego Zoo to the new Wild Animal Park, where they were released into a one-hundred-acre enclosure. Frankly, I think they were moved there out of administrative frustration at their failure to breed and unseemly displays. I suspect there might also have been the secret hope that coyotes might eat them and end their reign of vulgarity and terror. The coyotes failed to show up, and Charlie and Susie continued to look for ways to be a nuisance. There was still a lot of construction work going on in association with opening the park. Typically, we would consider this activity to be disturbing to the natural behaviors of wild animals, but that was not what happened. Charlie and Susie quickly established themselves as supervisors, seeming to be more intent in preventing work than encouraging it. And, in a surprisingly quiet manner, they added one more behavior and soon became the proud parents of a newly hatched hornbill.

To me, this change of behavior was fascinating! They had been together for twenty years and had done nothing but court. Then all of a sudden, they were baby makers. At age sixteen, I had some powerful urges to at least dabble in making babies myself, so the only part of Charlie I could not understand was what took so long and why he hadn't been interested in Susie before this. That got me curious about reproduction and, as if I needed an excuse, I decided I wanted to study what makes birds "do it." I was equally certain that whatever I learned could probably be applied to my thus far nonexistent dating life. It was in that light that I felt it was time to get serious about school.

Through all this—and despite my focused interest in animals and my well-earned reputation as a nerd—I was a C-average student. I was considered a nerd because I was always in the library. The reality was I was in the library to avoid the bullies who would steal my lunch (yes, even in high school) and to read about things that interested me, like animals. Sadly for my grade point average, animals had nothing to do with what I was in school for. It was always hard for me in an academic system that focused on everything except what I was interested in. It seemed like my dreams were bigger than my IQ.

Thankfully, there were a lot of special teachers who kept me going, teachers who kept the spark in me ignited and, wherever possible, worked to fan the flame. I would have given up in high school were it not for them. Everyone knew that if you wanted to be a scientist, you needed to take two years of algebra, and David Rightmer was my algebra teacher. Algebra made no sense to me, and struggle as I might, I simply could not figure it out. It was my second year of algebra, and I was going into final exams with a big fat D. My chances of flunking were huge. If that happened, I could resign myself to happily mopping floors and picking up trash for the rest of my life.

I will never forget when someone knocked on our front door the night before my final exam. When I answered, there stood my algebra teacher. "May I come in? You need to pass this exam tomorrow, and I am going to help you." He stayed late into the evening. The following day, I aced the algebra test, and better than that, I understood how I answered every question. It was exhilarating to finally believe I could do it.

Unfortunately, the algebra test was just one score among a litany of others and, collectively, not enough to get me into a state college or university, but it inspired me. I enrolled at a nearby junior college (a place we used to call "high school with ashtrays and little accountability") and planned on cleaning up my study habits as well as my GPA. But, distracted by my work at the Wild Animal Park and lots of hiking in the local open countryside, I continued to earn mediocre grades, and the prospect of further college education faded. By now, I was a keeper at the park and ready to settle for being the best keeper ever.

My parents had greater expectations, however. Dad had made it through college after a stint in the army, and my older brother and sister had long ago graduated with apparent ease. When it looked like I would be the first to disappoint my parents, they leveraged some help from an influential friend of the family who was associated with the University of California at San Diego. He told me, "I can get you in, but the only one who can keep you there is you." So I started my third struggling college year in a prestigious school on their most scientifically rigorous campus, Revelle.

As an upperclassman, I could take the classes I had always imagined would flip my switch. With algebra, organic chemistry, and biochemistry mostly in my rearview mirror, I could finally take a class on animals. There was a young, long-haired professor who was a herpetologist, someone who studies reptiles and amphibians, and I wasted no time signing up for his class.

In my small community of tiny box homes and trailers, the neighbors already considered me a local resource on snakes and lizards. I'd spent a lot of evenings and weekends with friends from the Wild Animal Park, driving on the roads of the nearby Anza Borrego Desert at night, collecting or observing snakes, lizards, scorpions, and spiders. In time, I had learned a lot about them, but I was anxious to learn more. I had never forgotten that four-eyed snake I had found in the backyard, and now I could get the whole story. I got to my first herpetology class early and sat dead center in the front row because I knew this was my academic moment, my breakthrough. The professor came in, turned on the overhead projector, and pulled his first sheet from his presentation folder. I leaned forward in eager anticipation of fabulous photos of strange and wondrous reptiles.

Once again, I was disappointed and more than a little confused. There was no picture of an interesting reptile, not one. Instead, it was a line map with bubbles and equations and something about territory size. With each subsequent image, I slid deeper into a chasm of confusing numbers and summations. How could someone be a herpetologist and do all their studies sitting in their office remote from the real creatures by fiddling with mathematical equations? I got the feeling that this guy had never even seen a real lizard. The concept of studying an animal without ever seeing it or touching it seemed counterintuitive to me. I wanted to be the biologist trudging in a forest, rescuing animals, and making the world right again. By the time the class let out, all I could think was, "What the hell was he talking about?"

My biology heroes were people like Farley Mowat, the Canadian biologist and author (*Never Cry Wolf*) who had lived with the wolves, and Konrad Lorenz, an Austrian scientist and the father of the science of ethology, or the study of natural behaviors in the wild. Mr. Mowat was funny. He could weave a story and loved sharing the wonders of the Canadian north. Dr. Lorenz wrote about science in a way I could understand, shared a Nobel Prize in 1973, and later in my life, he even turned out to be a pretty good pen pal. But this was not what I was experiencing in school. None of my studies even began to approach my passions, and I was more convinced than ever that I really was not up to this. Maybe science and academics simply were not what I thought they were. I didn't sign on to study circles and arrows and graphs and charts. I wanted to learn about nature and how it worked, not statistically where all the successes and failures were averaged out, but more intimately where you witnessed the cost and benefits, new life and death.

I was only two years away from a degree in biology and hoped I had it in me to finish. Then I could settle into that keeper job at the Park, go to parties, hand-raise gorillas, and chase snakes and girls—the good life. I struggled mightily for the first and second academic quarters and then gave up on UCSD. In a frustrated last-ditch effort, I leveraged the fact that I was in the UC system and put in a request to transfer to UC Davis for the third quarter of my junior year. Luck was on my side. With my family's support and the zoo's blessing and promise of holiday work, I transferred to UC Davis to study avian biology. UC Davis had veterinary medicine, which meant they must have animals. They also had wildlife and fisheries management, which sounded close to something I would like. I would give academics one last shot, but this time at my dream campus.

UC Davis turned out to be, in so many ways, the perfect institution for me. Everyone at UCSD was searching for answers with an electron microscope or in complex mathematical constructs. UC Davis had all of that and a strong farm and agriculture program, along with wildlife management programs that not only included living breathing animals with their bodies still intact, but the study of their habits and habitats as well.

There was an intoxicating freshness about being in a great school, taking classes that seemed relevant, and being led through academia by a caring undergraduate professor, Dr. Frank Ogasawara. Dr. O studied things like artificial insemination in double-breasted turkeys, sperm nests, and artificial sperm storage. Among other things, I admired him for having published an article in *National Geographic* magazine, stemming from his fascination with Japanese long-tailed fowl and his interest in oncology. The tail feathers of the long-tailed fowl never stopped growing, which provided fodder for his studies in cancer as well as a very traditional job for people in Japan whose responsibility it was to hold the chickens' tails out of the dirt while they walked around. At night, the roosters were placed on their perches and their tails gently hung on hooks to keep them off the ground. This was the first time I'd had a professor who actually wanted to meet me, know what I was up to, and who considered it his job to help me. He was one of the kindest, most caring men I have ever met.

The campus was closed to cars and dominated by a huge crush of bicycles, resulting in surprisingly few crashes. I really felt at home and was finally academically inspired. The change academically was similar to my social experience of going from my high school, where I was a bit of a misfit, to my job with like-minded friends. After midterms in my first quarter, I was looking at straight A's. Straight A's at the school of my dreams was absolutely unbelievable. My low C-average history now seemed a thing of the past.

Excited about my scholastic success, I headed into a three-day holiday weekend determined to celebrate. I partied hard with friends at the dorm. We did all the things you might expect of science undergrads. We were playing some sort of cops and robbers game and doing a bit of drinking when I fell down a flight of stairs. No big deal; I had drunk a fair amount of alcohol and therefore felt little pain. After my roommates headed out to be with their families for the weekend, I limped off to bed. Several hours later, I woke with excruciating pain in my ankle. I was in paralyzing pain, the kind where any attempt at moving caused deep, immobilizing, nauseating stabs of pain. This was way back when phones were not in your pocket but actually hung on the wall. I leveraged myself out of bed and onto the floor and tried to reach the phone to call someone for help. I couldn't do it. Horrible waves of pain and nausea rolled through me each time I moved. Try as I might, I was trapped and incapacitated. In the end, I realized I had no choice but to wait on the floor until one of my roommates returned two days later. He walked into an unpleasant scene. I'd had nothing to eat or drink since they left, had been sick to my stomach, and was unable to get to a bathroom. It was not a pretty situation.

My roommate showed far more compassion than I would have expected, given my condition. He scooped me up and rushed me to the campus hospital, where the heinous Nurse Ratched from *One Who Flew Over the Cuckoo's Nest* apparently spent her holidays. After a perfunctory look, she told me I had only sprained my ankle and not so subtly mentioned that I ought to grow up. I was unceremoniously delivered back to my friends with nothing more than an Ace bandage to show for all the pain and heroics.

Despite the fine care from the nurse and a sincere effort at following her advice, the fact was I could not function at all. The pain was unbearable, and that made it hard to eat and impossible to walk or ride a bike to class. Days into the second half of the quarter, Dr. O called to find out why I was not in class, and the whole tragic story spilled out. Literally, the next thing I knew, there was an ambulance parked outside the dorm and medics trotting up the stairs to my room. This time, when I arrived at the hospital, an actual doctor looked at my ankle under Dr. O's close supervision. After examining x-rays with Dr. O, a specialist was brought in from San Francisco and began the slow process of proper treatment and healing. But this story was less about my ankle and more about Dr. O. With me fully incapacitated and final exams on the horizon, he attended my classes for me and took meticulous notes. At the end of the day, after all my classes, he would come to the hospital, read his notes to me, and quiz me. When it was time for finals, he rearranged the dates to give me time to rest in between and drove me to every exam, where he had an easy chair set up for me to sit in. To put this in context, Dr. Ogasawara was a full professor. He had teaching responsibilities as well as research obligations. Now, every day, he was going to my classes then taking the same amount of time to come back and read the notes to me and test me. I finished the quarter with my new GPA intact. Again, an amazing teacher touched my life. Thank you, Dr. Ogasawara.

Thanks to a system that worked and taught to my interests, I excelled in my final year of undergraduate work. At precisely that time, K.C. Lint retired from his position as curator of birds for the San Diego Zoo. I had applied for his job when I was eight years old. Why not try it now that I was a mature and educated twenty-one? For the second time, I was passed over for the job. It was crushing. K.C. Lint had held the position for decades, and the same could be expected of the new curator. My dream was likely over, killed by a guy named Art Risser who had graduated from UC Davis only a few years ahead of me. I found solace in my academic success. My grades were finally good enough to ignite the dream of pressing on and going to graduate school.

Chapter 5

GRADUATE SCHOOL

"Obstacles are those frightful things you see when
you take your eyes off your goal."
~HENRY FORD

With the curator spot at the zoo filled, I stepped through the next door to explore graduate school. I needed more than good grades; I needed a professor who would take me on as a student and a lab to work in. Perhaps, I should not have been surprised that on an agricultural campus in a department that focused on chickens and turkeys, professors studying the sex life of wild birds were, as they say, "rare as hen's teeth." Apparently, the real money was in chickens and turkeys if you were interested in bird sex. While semen collection and sperm storage had their fascinating aspects (did you know that poultry have sperm storage ducts and can save sperm for a long time?), it was not my cup of tea. Mine was a much more esoteric interest. I wanted to study the motivations behind the sex life of exotic birds, like zebra finches. I wanted to know why they had sex and, from a conservation and recovery standpoint, why they wouldn't have sex. Finally, if they were not inclined to have sex, how were they ultimately convinced to give in? It seemed to me this could be important information with potentially broad applications that might well include my dating life.

I finally found a professor interested in sex in wild birds. Dr. D. Michael Fry split his teaching and research time between UC Berkeley and UC Davis. Sadly for me, his interest was not in zebra finches. Instead, he had a grant from the federal government to study the causes of reproductive failure in the California condor, our continent's largest flying bird and North America's most endangered species. Almost begrudgingly, I joined his laboratory and set about learning about the California condor and birds that were closely related. Unknown to me at the time, this failure to find a zebra finch aficionado would forever alter the trajectory of my career and my life.

To determine the reproductive state of birds, we had to be able to track hormone cycles, and because we wanted to track cycles in wild birds, we had to do it in the least intrusive way possible. If you want to look at a person's hormones, you can draw blood. But looking at hormone breakdown products or hormone metabolites in our urine is less invasive and gives similar results. In order to sample metabolites, all you need to do is give your doctor a urine sample, but birds are not that easy. It turns out that flying requires a lot of energy, and the heavier you are, the more energy it takes to keep you in the air. (Keep this in mind as we insist on wider seats on airliners... just saying.) It turns out that birds have given up a lot in order to fly, which seriously complicates their sex life. Some of the stuff they gave up seems pretty important, like a penis, for example. Many bones have been reduced or eliminated entirely. While our heads sit on two bones called occipital condyles, rounded knobs on the occipital bone, birds trimmed the number of condyles from two to one. With their heads sitting on only one point, they can turn their heads much further than we can. Other bones are hollow. They have no teeth; their beaks are thin, lightweight, and hollow; and they have no sweat glands or bladders. But wait, as I mentioned, they don't have a penis. If that alone was not bad enough, their testicles and ovaries literally disappear most of the year. Nature seemingly had asked, "If you are not using them, why carry them around?" This all begins to hint at why there might be some problems getting the engine started each time spring rolls around, but we digress. Along with all the other things that were too heavy, nature decided that extra water and a bladder to hold it was just too much weight. So birds don't make urine; instead, they produce a white pasty waste called uric acid. Then they combine outlets for sperm, eggs, uric acid, and feces into one convenient hole called a cloaca. I know this may seem like too much information, but if you are like a lot of people who wish they could fly, this might help you get over it. For us in the laboratory, all these issues with weight meant we needed fecal samples, not urine samples, to follow hormone cycles in condors.

When you are studying an endangered species, there are a whole lot of reasons not to experiment directly on the species in question. It is smart to use a surrogate, and to do that, you need to take a lot of things into consideration. Ideally, the surrogate is a closely related species with similar physiology and behavior. The more common the surrogate is, the better, as this allows you to have a large number of specimens to work with.

In the Americas, there are seven species of closely related New World vultures. Collectively, they are fascinating birds, completely unrelated to hawks, eagles, and other birds of prey, and even more surprisingly, unrelated to Old World vultures. The New World vultures are an evolutionary branch with links back to storks and flamingos, while the Old World vultures have branched off from the true birds of prey. The overall similarity of New World and Old World vultures is an elegant example of convergent evolution, where two unrelated types of animals evolve to look alike because of their exploitation of similar environmental niches.

The Old World vultures of Europe, Asia, and Africa are perhaps best known from National Geographic or BBC Nature films showing them aggressively piling up at large carcasses protected by lions, hyenas, or other large predators. Between the vultures and other scavengers, a carcass of a buffalo or bear will literally disappear in the course of a day.

When it comes to a direct comparison of Old World and New World vultures, there are some interesting tidbits. If you stand to the side of any New World vulture, you can see in one nostril and out the other. Better them than us. Theirs is known as a perforate nostril, while the Old World vultures have a rather more attractive (to people) imperforate nostril, which you cannot see all the way through. There are many other differences, but one of the more fascinating and important to this story is the behavior of urohidrosis. The roots of the word urohidrosis are found in the Ancient Greek words for sweat and urine. While it is one thing for birds to give up certain organs like bladders, teeth, and sweat glands, their bodies still need to have a mechanism for performing those basic functions. Urohidrosis allows vultures to rid themselves of the pasty uric acid from their kidneys and spray it on their legs to replace sweat glands and regulate body temperature. Pretty darn efficient and ingenious. Interestingly, this is a behavior shared with storks and flamingos (along with perforate nostrils) and not with the Old World vultures. What this all means is that you can almost think of New World vultures as ugly flamingoes that eat roadkill.

The bottom line was that studying the far more numerous Old World vultures would not be relevant, nor would studying any of the hawks or eagles. For the California condor, it either needed to be another New World vulture or perhaps a stork. Among the New

World vultures, the Andean condor was the most similar, but they too were an endangered species. While there were quite a few of them in zoos, I needed something closer to our lab and with fewer legal restrictions. Next up was the turkey vulture, not quite a condor but better than a stork or flamingo and good enough.

Our lab was going to need to set up a small group of captive turkey vultures so that we could consistently follow individuals' hormone cycles throughout the year. Building the pens was the easy part, but then we had to recruit their residents. Proud of my childhood skills at catching skunks and possums, I happily took on the task of catching a few turkey vultures. How hard could it be anyway? Every good trapper knows you need a trap, some bait, and the right place to put it. Then you just show up later and collect your animals.

UC Davis was surrounded by agricultural fields of alfalfa, rice, tomatoes, corn, and more. There were areas with ranches and free-roaming cattle, sheep, and goats. Alfalfa harvesting seemed to kill a lot of small mammals, and turkey vultures would often follow the big mowers and harvesters. The abundance of chopped vermin made it impossible to guess where the vultures might go. It seemed like finding a big carcass that the birds would visit regularly over a few days was a better way to go. It occurred to me that one of the cattle or goat ranches might be a good site. There were always the afterbirths from calving and the occasional mortality from disease or predators. However, ranchers didn't want disease or more predators than they had and, as a result, were nearly fanatical about picking up carcasses and waste to avoid attracting wild animals or spreading disease. So, in the end, these larger, dead ranch animals were less plentiful, and we decided to use roadkill, which was nearly ubiquitous.

Now we had a study species and bait, but it turned out that turkey vultures were way smarter than you might think and quite challenging to trap. Whereas the Old World vultures were famous for their voraciousness at a carcass, New World vultures were finicky and almost dainty at a carcass. Like many people, when I would see circling vultures in the sky, I would assume there was something dead below them, and therefore, it must be a good place to try and trap them. Sadly, this was another Hollywood myth. It was quite unlikely that they were circling because they had found food and far more likely that they were testing out thermals and preparing to move on in their search for the next meal. Scouting for vultures perching in trees or walking on the ground was a far more productive way of determining where they might be feeding.

Turkey vultures are quite unusual when it comes to locating food. Most birds search for food visually, while some, like owls, depend on specialized hearing to locate prey. Consistent with other anatomical changes for flight, birds have reduced parts of the brain not absolutely required for survival (hence the term "bird brain"), but the turkey vulture is unusual because it has a very well-developed olfactory bulb, which allows them to locate dead animals by detecting the chemical ethyl mercaptan released by decaying flesh. Ethyl mercaptan is the odor that gas companies add to the natural gas piped into your home because natural gas is odorless and could be extremely dangerous if it leaked into your home undetected. In the late 1930s and into the 1940s, field engineers with the Union Oil Company of California infused gas lines with high concentrations of ethyl mercaptan to help locate leaks in the lines. They simply upped the amount of odor in the lines and watched to see where the turkey vultures landed.

Having grown up in a rural community, I had learned to set traps for everything from gophers to bobcats, but a soaring vulture really was going to require more thought. We finally settled on using a modified bal-chatri noose. In our case, it was basically a carpet of monofilament nooses tied to a wire mesh. We buried the mesh with the nearly invisible nooses sticking up above the soil line. This was done right along a country road. We would use one of the nooses to secure whatever odiferous roadkill we could find in the area. Then when the vulture stepped into the noose, it would tighten, and we would have him.

Despite my interest in dating, this was a bad time for me. I had a 1972 Volkswagen bug, and I spent my evenings and early mornings driving the roads looking for dead animals. Anything bigger than a squirrel was good—possums, raccoons, and even skunks. Volkswagens did not have much of a trunk, so each carcass was bagged and thrown into the backseat. Like my time with the billy goats in the Animal Care Center, I found that olfactory amnesia was really convenient unless you picked up a date and didn't know what your car smelled like.

Once the bal-chatri noose was set up, I would hide in the bushes and wait. It turned out that of all the vultures, turkey vultures were the shyest. They were extremely wary about approaching carcasses. I spent a lot of days hiding in the bushes, breathing air that reeked of dead animals, while absolutely nothing happened because something unknown to me was out of place to the vultures. They had spectacular eyesight, and if they detected activity, it would condemn that location for the rest of the day. So any need by me to leave my hiding place for a bathroom break or a stretch simply meant the day was over.

I finally caught my first turkey vulture, but it was with mixed feelings of success and disgust. The vulture drifted down onto the ground near the carcass and trap. Over nearly an hour, he simply wandered around inspecting the body but not getting too close. Finally, he approached and took his first bite of succulent, rotten flesh. He fed for quite a long time. Even though he was unaware of the nooses, it was uncanny how successful he was at avoiding them. Other than fearing that I would not catch him, the long feeding didn't worry me. Vultures gorge if they can when they feed, rapidly getting as much food as possible into their crop. Having given up so many seemingly important organs to fly, the behavior of gorging and adding a lot of weight seems counterintuitive. They needed a backup plan for emergencies when getting off the ground quickly was critical. To accomplish this, they were all too willing to unload a crop full of fetid flesh and offal in order to take flight in a hasty manner. As soon as I saw a noose close around his leg, I rushed from my hiding spot to claim my prize. Hoping he could escape by losing some weight, he covered me in putrid debris. Needless to say, I nearly lightened my weight as well.

This was my first capture. As fetidly smelly and damp as I was, I was also very happy and proud. I drove directly to my professor's home to share the news. Sadly, I have never felt so unwelcome in my life. Dr. Fry was a social animal, and he had guests that day for a late afternoon get-together. I never made it past the front porch.

Though it never got easier, I finally ended up with a small population of turkey vultures and a notebook full of data from their waste.

Chapter 6

FLYCATCHERS
Catch My
INTEREST

"Follow the wandering, the distraction, find out why the mind has wandered; pursue it, go into it fully. When the distraction is completely understood, then that particular distraction is gone. When another comes, pursue it also."
-JIDDU KRISHNAMURTI

There were distractions from my work. I had to pay the bills. A weekend or two here and there picking up trash in San Diego wasn't doing it. I took on the job of assistant manager at Sycamore Lane Apartments, and though the pay was awful, I got my rent for free. As students moved out, I fixed the holes they left in the walls and replaced the shower walls that every one of them destroyed.

Each morning before school, I would check on the two pools, clean out the skimmers, and make sure all was well. One morning, while making my rounds, I discovered a tiny pink blob of a bird lying on the sidewalk. Probably one of the many cats in the complex had disturbed a nest and somehow overlooked this tiny, featherless baby. It was too small for me to identify the exact species, but baby birds, regardless of species, required protein to grow, which was how canned cat food became a staple for this little bird. As he grew and began to feather out, I was finally able to identify him as a flycatcher, specifically a western kingbird. In a funny way, this little bird would open another important facet of my future.

I enjoyed my time working with a bird closer to my original love. While not a finch, a flycatcher was far from being a vulture. Recognizing that he would have to learn to catch prey on his own, I knew I needed to help him hone his hunting skills before releasing him. On warm summer days, dragonflies decorated the tips of car antennas in the parking lot like so many bobbleheads. I learned I could approach the dragonfly with a rolled-up newspaper and could stun it and knock it to the ground with a quick slap. I would tie a thread to one of its legs. As the dazed dragonfly recovered its senses, it would find itself flying in circles around the inside of my apartment on a leash with a baby flycatcher in full pursuit.

I was impressed when the little kingbird went from his diet of wet, canned cat food to dragonflies right up until I thought I had killed him. A day or two after his diet change, he started out lethargic and sat on the back of the couch, looking a bit dejected. Suddenly, he began to cough and convulse. Out of his little beak came a huge ball of dragonfly parts. All the indigestible chitinous exoskeletons of the insects came out in surprisingly large, hard balls. It turned out this was all normal, just a flycatcher's way of discarding the indigestible parts. This first time, we were both surprised.

Dubbed Tyrone because of his scientific name (*Tyrannus vertica-lis*), my little bird became quite the hunter. The day came when it was time for him to go outside and fend for himself. I popped him into a tree and went on about my business. Tyrone was going to have none of this. He followed me doggedly, landing on my head or shoulders. At first, I tried to discourage this, but then my affection for my new friend took over. If I walked to class, I would slap at bushes with a walking stick. If a bug flew out, Tyrone would sally out from my shoulder, catch the insect, and land on my shoulder again, where he would proceed to beat the poor bug to death against my shoulder or head. When I arrived at class, I would grab Tyrone and toss him into a tree and head inside. After class, all it took was a little whistle from me, and he would show up from wherever he had wandered off to. We would head back to our apartment, hunting and whistling along the way.

Several of my classmates were falconers, who hunted birds and rabbits with their falcons. My love of vultures made me somewhat of an outcast, but once I had my hunting kingbird, people at least smiled at me. Don't worry; I knew it was a sad smile, but at least I was noticed.

No matter how hard I tried to force Tyrone to make his own life in the wild, he kept coming back. I decided that if I housed Tyrone with my flock of vultures in their large flight cage where he couldn't follow me when I left, maybe he would develop some independence. This went on into the summer. By early fall, the other western flycatchers were leaving the Davis area for the winter, so now was the time. One evening when Tyrone was asleep, I went to the cage in the dark, took him outside the pen, settled him onto a branch, and left.

Our vultures were only fed every few days, and so I did not need to go back to the cages for several days. When I did, I searched around for Tyrone. He was gone. He had either gotten lost looking for me, been eaten, or far less likely, integrated back into the migrating population of flycatchers and moved on. I was afraid that I would never really know the answer to how it ended. Suspecting that he had probably been eaten, I was happier going forward in ignorance.

In early spring the following year, I spotted a small group of western kingbirds at the vulture pens. On a lark, I gave a whistle, and to my surprise, one of the kingbirds stopped, cocked his head at me, and then flew to a nearby bush. We exchanged whistles, and he stayed in the area but did not come to me. It had to be Tyrone. It had to be that I had successfully reintroduced an animal back to the wild, which was exhilarating.

Chapter 7

The
CALIFORNIA
CONDOR
Closeup

"If you think something is ugly, look harder.
Ugliness is just a failure of seeing."

~MATT HAIG, The Humans

My graduate professor and I had a relationship that ran the gamut. We enjoyed each other and were passionate about our work. But the eternal battle was always there. He worked in a lab, and I wanted to be in the field. He wanted to do gel electrophoresis, and I wanted to watch a condor glide on a thermal. We argued about what specifically my project should be. We argued about how it should be done and how our results should be interpreted. We could argue about whether it was day or night. He was the professor, and he most often won the arguments. There was never a clean win for me. Only years later did I realize he was teaching me an important lesson. What I really learned was how to constructively argue a point. How to research a position, understand it inside and out, and finally, how to defend it. This has turned out to be the single most useful and productive skill that I took away from school, a skill for which I will always thank Dr. D. Michael Fry. Nevertheless, our endless debates led to tension in the lab. When we finally had accomplished as much as we could reasonably do studying our turkey vultures, we were ready for the target species—the California condor. Permits came allowing us to collect feces from a wild condor. The task fell to me, and with all the tension in the lab, it could not have come at a better time.

For several years, people had monitored behaviors and taken samples from a California condor named Topa Topa that was housed at the Los Angeles Zoo. Topa Topa was the only California condor in captivity, and people had already studied him up one side and down the other. So my first task was to increase our sample size and acquire fecal samples from wild condors. Easy right? In the beginning, the process was far more difficult than I had imagined it would be, but it burned into my psyche a permanent and vivid definition of the term "endangered."

The original range of the condor was literally coast to coast in North America. The constriction of its range began in the late Pleistocene, possibly associated with the disappearance of many large mammals, which were most certainly their preferred source of carrion. In all my years of watching condors, I never saw them on roadkill like squirrels or rabbits. They had a distinct preference for large carcasses. Early settlers killing off huge herds of buffalo and other large vertebrates did not do much for the condor either. By the mid-1900s, California was all that was left for the condor.

But why California? Particularly Southern California, where they resided immediately adjacent to Los Angeles, the largest and most polluted city in the state? At one point, a theory was put forward that California was the equivalent of a black hole for condors, and that was why they were in California and going extinct. This might take some explaining. Habitats, like your neighborhood, have a carrying capacity—a maximum number of lives that can be supported within that neighborhood or ecosystem. As condors died in California, new birds may have moved there to fill the vacancies, they then died, and the cycle repeated. So while a first reaction was to assume they were only in California because it was the best place for them, it was conceivable that the exact opposite could also be true. If their decline was solely because of the disappearance of large animals in the Pleistocene, then why were they still here thousands of years later? Let's just say that the last fifteen thousand years or so had clearly been hard on them, and there was a lot that we did not understand about their decline.

By the time I was in the field, it was estimated that there were only twenty to twenty-four California condors surviving in the rugged foothills of Southern California. They ranged through Ventura, Santa Barbara, Riverside, Los Angeles, and San Luis Obispo counties. As their names implied, many of these counties were home to major metropolitan centers. While I was still quite uninformed in the ways of the condor, I knew better than to start my search in or near one of these big cities. I was one of those guys who seldom read the instructions before trying to put the bicycle together. I was always anxious to hurry up and get something done and would tell anyone who asked (and many who didn't) that I was quite an expert in the field. In this particular search, though, a little bit of research and prior planning would have helped a great deal in the execution. Due to that lack of planning, my collection trip to Southern California started what would turn into a very long summer.

Condors were big, or so I had heard, and so I headed into the field quite certain that they would be hard to miss. I did a lot of hiking under the summer sun and wandered into areas I had no business being in. I camped, fished, and in the end, got extremely frustrated as I recognized the odds of going back to school with some condor feces were getting slimmer and slimmer with each passing day. Still following my male ego, instead of stopping for a moment to ask for directions, I decided one day to climb to the top of a mountain, where I would have a wider view all around me. Certainly, if I just sat there long enough, I would at least see a condor, though I knew in my heart of hearts that seeing one was a long way from getting one to defecate somewhere where I could take a sample.

I began the challenging climb up a steep mountainside in thick, scratchy, heavily scented sage bushes. It was late summer and very hot and dry. The exertion associated with climbing the steep hillside combined with the weight of my pack made me hot, tired, soaked with sweat, and a little cranky. As I neared the ridgeline, the dry, scratchy chaparral brush gave way to loose scree, where I was exposed to the full effect of the sun. Although I could feel the warm draft pushing up the hot mountainside behind me, it wasn't enough to keep me on my feet, so I crawled through the loose rock and gravel. Some twenty feet before summiting the ridge, a shadow fell across me. I was not sure if it was goosebumps or a shiver from being so suddenly shaded, but I felt the shadow more than saw it. On my hands and knees, I looked up directly into the eyes of a California condor—a bird with a wingspan of nine feet. This huge bird, maybe thirty to forty feet above my head, had crossed the ridge from the opposite side in search of the same warm, rising thermal I had felt pushing me up my side of the mountain. Without moving its wings, the condor simply rotated the long individual primary feathers at the end of each wing just enough to let the wind slip between them and came to a mid-air stop, turned its head, and looked at me. Our eyes met. It was an amazing moment. I couldn't say we communicated, but we each certainly ran a fast analysis of each other. I had never seen any bird park in the air. The condor did not move at all except maybe a subtle tilting of its tail as it adjusted in the thermal. It simply hung in one place as if on invisible strings.

I froze. I did not want to do anything to end this moment. The wind at my back was warm and whispered as it gained speed against the mountain. For a moment, I felt transported back in time. It was the bird, me, and nothing else. I kept my eyes locked on the condor. I did not want to miss any movement. Like my scientific hero Konrad Lorenz, I was witnessing raw nature up close. I felt like I was part of the BBC Nature series. Most of all, I felt privileged to be in a secret world that was just ours, mine and the condor's. I was finally home.

Once the bird was satisfied with whatever information it had gained, those long, elegant feathers rotated back into place, and the thermal it had so deftly located lifted the condor rapidly away. Elevated by these thermals, a condor would float up for miles, until to the naked eye it "dots out," disappearing from view. Once the condor had achieved its desired altitude, it could slip off the rising air currents. In a controlled descending glide, they could cover miles and miles of ground at speeds of more than 50 mph, only to find another thermal and repeat the process.

As I watched my first wild condor disappear into the blue sky, I came to understand a long-held Chumash belief. Native Americans of the California coast referred to the condor as Xolxol (pronounced hole-hole). They believed that when a person died, their spirit traveled to the world of the Sky People on the wings of a condor. They knew this could happen because they witnessed what I had just seen, the California condor disappearing into the Sky World. I was moved to my core, and now a species I previously had little interest in would be the center of my life.

Chapter 8

The
CALIFORNIA
CONDOR
Recovery Program

"Chance favors only the prepared mind."
~LOUIS PASTEUR

In 1979, the federal government formally adopted a plan from the California Condor Recovery Team, which included a captive breeding program. In a strange, serendipitous confluence of my varied experiences—running through the chaparral of Southern California, being a keeper at the San Diego Wild Animal Park, collecting feces and capturing wild vultures, chasing down condors, acquiring a master's degree from UC Davis, developing a strong and undeserved sense of confidence, and finding myself unemployed—I was uniquely prepared when my big chance arrived. My name popped up in the condor circles, and my big opportunity came in the form of a phone call from Dr. Arthur Risser, the guy who beat me out as the successor to K.C. Lint as curator of birds for the San Diego Zoo.

Art always looked younger than his years, almost boyish, but he possessed a brilliant mind with a wicked sense of humor, which he displayed in his first question. "Do you know how to hand-raise a California condor?" Art already knew the answer to his question. Of course, I didn't know how to hand-raise a California condor. Nobody did because nobody had ever done it. So, I said, "Yes, of course, I know how to hand-raise a California condor."

He hired me. My dad had always told me that the way to be the best in your field was to be the *only* person in your field, and I was instantly the best California condor keeper in the world. Interestingly enough, we didn't have any California condors, so my job was less about taking care of condors and more about learning as much as possible to prepare myself for the day when we did. The race to save the critically endangered bird was heating up, and I needed to be ready.

Because Art and I both knew that there was no way I actually knew how to hand-raise a condor, I was given free license to do whatever I needed to do to get ready. I'd learned a lot about preparedness from my awful experience catching turkey vultures, so I poured everything I had into preparation.

First off, I developed a working relationship with a keeper by the name of Augie Campos. Augie was the keeper in charge of the "string," or group of animals, that included the zoo's Andean condors. The Andean condor was a closely related but larger and sexually dimorphic condor from South America. Their keeper was a genuinely sweet older guy who had given the zoo the best he had over the years and now, as he approached retirement, was coasting.

The department was kind to him. It was pretty much understood that Augie would be left alone until he retired. There was a small shed in his area known as "Augie's shack," where we would check in regularly to make sure he was okay, and just as often, we had to check on his birds. One time, the supervisor found a dead bird in one of Augie's pens. He picked it up and took it for necropsy at the zoo hospital. For the next couple of weeks, every morning at coffee, he would always ask about the bird, and Augie would assure him it was fine and eating well. Nothing to worry about there!

Augie hadn't always been like this. He loved to talk about his past, which was why I insisted on being his friend. In earlier years, he had been one of K.C. Lint's prized keepers. Between 1942 and 1952, the Andean condors in Augie's care had produced viable eggs, and K.C. Lint had hatched and reared nine chicks from them. These were the first Andean condors ever raised in captivity. They had learned a lot about breeding condors and hand-rearing their offspring, but perhaps more importantly, they recorded the phenomenon of double-clutching. Andean condors in the wild typically laid one egg every two years. The egg took nearly two months to hatch. They would spend the next six months rearing that chick to the point of leaving the nest and nearly another year to self-sufficiency before the cycle repeated. What Augie and K.C. had discovered was that taking an egg away from the pair to artificially incubate would stimulate the birds to lay another egg, thereby doubling their reproductive rate. Furthermore, they learned that if they took the chick away for captive rearing, the adult pair would not skip a year of breeding. All in all, this meant the pair could be stimulated to quadruple their reproductive rate. The value of this information and how it might help the California condor was not lost on K.C. and the zoo's director, Belle Benchley.

These successes and the knowledge that they could influence reproductive rates had led K.C. Lint and Belle Benchley to propose a captive breeding program for the California condor as early as 1949. By 1952, the State of California issued permits to the zoo to capture California condors. Sadly, in an action that foreshadowed the actions of the 1980s, the National Audubon Society and their condor biologist Carl Koford threw a fit. In 1954, the permits were revoked before the zoo had successfully captured a condor. As K.C. Lint put it in a 1984 interview, the permits were revoked because the National Audubon Society's president and chief executive officer John Baker "...said he would rather see all the California condors die before he would want to see one in captivity. This was his philosophy."

The California condor had been recognized as an endangered species since the early 1900s and protected by federal law since 1967. But it wasn't until the passage of the Endangered Species Act (ESA) under President Richard Nixon in 1973 that such a designation had any real teeth. The ESA required the government to establish a diverse recovery team to develop and oversee the implementation of a recovery plan to bring a species back to self-sustaining numbers.

The first recovery plan for the condor was published in 1974 and was fully focused on saving the condor from extinction through a series of land acquisitions and prohibitions of human activities ("acquire, restrict and protect"), retrospectively a typical and very traditional approach to conservation.

This plan was developed with no in-depth information on causes of death, and therefore, only touched lightly on poisoning associated with predator control. It made no mention of lead poisoning or a captive breeding program. It did, however, call out the lack of solid data and, probably because of that, focused almost exclusively on purchasing land and restricting human access. If effectively implemented, this approach had every reason to succeed as long as humans—their presence, their needs, and their politics—were not involved. Sadly, when conservation fails to recognize the human component, things can go drastically wrong as people attempt to protect their livelihoods and their checkbooks. One example of conservation through restriction going wrong took place in Florida, where bald eagle nest sites were protected from development. The simplest solution left for a land developer was to go and shoot the nesting pair and proceed with construction once there was no longer an active nest site. Things quickly headed in a similar direction for the condor. In presenting the first approved version of a recovery plan, Lynn Greenwalt, the director of the US Fish and Wildlife Service, described the tone of the plan as "somewhat defensive." He went on to say, "We have no apologies to make for the fact that the welfare of the condor conflicts with economic interests." Clearly, the stage was set for a battle, and there was no time wasted before the first shots were fired. From the solid and well-recognized National Audubon Society to the more radical and inflammatory Friends of the Earth, the new plan was targeted and challenged.

Before you can take any meaningful steps to save a species, you first need to know why the species is in decline—identifying the problem or problems is an essential step in solving them. A single condor could cover more than one hundred miles in rugged terrain in the course of a day. Without radio tags, it was difficult to know where they were going and what they encountered on their journeys. It was even harder to find a dead condor in this essentially trackless wilderness area. The dead condors we did find were very rare and strictly by chance. Radio telemetry to track their activities was the obvious solution, and the proposal was simple: trap birds, fit them with radio telemetry, and release them again. By tracking the birds, we would learn a great deal about how and where they spent their days, where they nested, roosted, and fed, and if a bird died, we would be able to find it and hopefully determine the cause of death.

As arguments raged on about how or even if the condor should be studied, much less saved, the condor population quietly continued its precipitous drop. It soon became clear that the decline of the condor would not be halted quickly enough through traditional conservation measures. Contingency plans were rapidly developed and promoted by the California Condor Recovery Team. One of the most controversial elements was the captive breeding of the condors by California-based zoos. The recovery team, along with staff from the FWS Captive Breeding Facility in Patuxent, Maryland, put together a plan for accelerated research in captive breeding in the hopes of rapid implementation. After a contentious review and with the support from the American Ornithological Union (now the American Ornithological Society), the FWS approved captive breeding as part of the recovery plan in February 1979. With the San Diego Zoo's broad reputation, specific expertise with Andean condors, and a long-held interest in California condors, they were an obvious choice as a captive breeding facility. Art Risser knew this and, forever a strategic thinker, wanted everything in place. Hiring me as a bird keeper was an early move in this process.

Perhaps the oddest thing about the battles to save the California condor was that conservation groups, such as the Sierra Club, the National Audubon Society, and Friends of the Earth, seemed to constantly stand in opposition to recovery. The battles had little to do with sound science and more to do with money, public relations, emotion, and the eloquent turn of phrase. On all these fronts, the activist groups were more effective than the dry, factual presentations by the recovery team scientists. With these tools and rants like "death with dignity," the Sierra Club, Earth First, and the Audubon Society were winning the battle for public opinion and stalling forward progress. By burning time, they were steadily driving the condor closer to the brink of extinction. One of the most eloquent and vocal activists was David Brower, the disgruntled executive director of the Sierra Club, who went on to found Friends of the Earth, best known as FOE. On the topic of radio telemetry, he summed up his position by writing, "What the world does not need is a flying Pleistocene radio station." Colorful as it was inaccurate, it was sadly effective and chewed up years of time while more condors died.

While I was still studying at UC Davis, I met and married Cyndi Kuehler. She was attractive, intensely intelligent, and a great student. I nearly ruined my grade point average by signing up for classes she was in so I could be around her. Ultimately, she worked in Dr. Fry's lab, studying the effects of DDT on eggshell thinning. She became a proficient oologist, a person who studies eggs. While I was working on condor behavior and the rearing of chicks, Cyndi was unknowingly positioning herself as the best person to oversee the incubation of their eggs.

Following up on the work of Augie Campos and my childhood hero K.C. Lint, Cyndi incubated the eggs of Andean condors, and I used Mr. Lint's notes from the 1940s as we refined techniques for hand-rearing them. Many years later, while surfing the internet, I found an interview with K.C. Lint that nearly brought tears to my eyes. Edmund Bajet at San Diego State University interviewed K.C. and asked him how his accomplishments were recognized by the zoo. He replied, "Well, you know, this is real interesting because way back, we raised the first Andean condors in captivity from 1942 to 1952. We raised nine of them. I kept very detailed notes on feeding and diets. So, when Bill Toone hatched their first California condor, I took all my notes over to him, and he used the same information, which is very interesting because that was a long time ago, forty-two years ago, when I pioneered the condor raising business. This is a form of recognition." These words meant the world to me, and I am so sorry that I was not aware of them until after his death. One of my heroes was honored that I used his knowledge. It can't get much better than that.

For the condor program, Cyndi and I were a good team. She knew how to hatch eggs, and I knew how to raise birds, but little would happen in this program if we couldn't hatch eggs. Cyndi and I had both been published in scientific journals as graduate students, so when we were married, she decided to continue using her maiden name. Because of our work with condors, our profile within the zoo grew, and perhaps we were gossiped about. The end result was that someone in power learned we were married. At that time, being married and working in the same department was considered very inappropriate. The zoo had a longstanding but terribly outdated nepotism rule that said married people could not work together. Cyndi had been hired a day or two after me, and therefore, was considered the junior employee and summarily terminated. Cyndi and I were personally quite pragmatic about the decision, but it seemed shortsighted on the part of the zoo. I would learn in due course the glitches inherent in the pedantic nature of corporate decision-making.

This disrupted carefully laid plans not only within the bird department but, even more importantly, for the national recovery plans for the condor. Now Art Risser's negotiating skills were going to be put to the test. He was, of course, cautious in his discussions with Cyndi and me, but through our conversations, two things became clear. He would not directly buck the system on our behalf, but he would support us if we could find a way around the nepotism rule. With the high-profile condor program developing rapidly, both of our distinctly different skill sets were needed. Cyndi and I quickly saw the obvious hole in the policy and took a quick trip across the border to Mexico and got a Mexican divorce. We came home with a very official-looking document loaded with red ribbons, impressive stamps, and seals and turned it into the human resources department. At no small risk to his own position within the zoo, Art Risser stepped up and rehired Cyndi, and we all got back to work.

Chapter 9

LEARNING
the
ROPES

"Alone we can do so little; together we can do so much."
-HELEN KELLER

Officially, the recovery program was set up as a collaboration between the United States Fish and Wildlife Service (USFWS), California Department of Fish and Game (CDFG), the Audubon Society, the Los Angeles Zoo, and the San Diego Zoo. The federal and state agencies were responsible for work in the field with assistance from the Audubon Society, and the zoos would be responsible for birds in captivity. But it was essential that the program be seamless with complete collaboration by all parties. For the most part, that worked. When I wasn't hatching and rearing baby Andean condors at the zoo, I was out in the field with Dr. Noel Snyder from USFWS and the California condors. It was a fascinating time, camping in the condor habitat and observing the birds as they searched for food, nested, raised their chicks, and spent leisurely days preening and resting in the sun. Noel was the lead biologist for the federal government's program to save the condor. He was the most focused and scientifically disciplined person I had ever met. He was bearded, brilliant, and determined. Hikes with Noel included huge distances in brutal scrub, treacherous terrain, and extreme temperatures. He sighed a lot but moved with the slow determination of a bulldozer. He had an equally slow, plodding, and thoughtful way of speaking. No one I had ever met could make my name take so long to say. When he would call my home or office, it would always be the same introductory statement, "Hello Bill ... this is Noel." That call could come at any time of day or night. It only mattered that at that moment, Noel needed to talk to you. In many cases, it was more that he needed to talk at you instead of to you. It was as if he needed to verbalize his arguments and thoughts so he could better hear and polish them. At times, the calls were frequent, long, and often in the wee hours, but they were always a privilege to be part of.

Most people did not know it, but he was also a talented cellist with a degree in music who had gone on to get a PhD in ornithology from Cornell University. He struck me as a true renaissance man. When I first met Noel, I only knew that he was in charge of the federal portion of the condor program. We enjoyed each other, and our relationship slowly grew. One day in his house in Ojai, right at the edge of the condor habitat, I went to the refrigerator to get a drink. There was a photo of Noel in a tuxedo playing his cello stuck to the door. I was surprised because I was sure he only owned jeans and rugged outdoor shirts with boots worn down by years in the field. His wife, Helen, saw me looking at the photo and gave me a profound insight into Noel. "He does one thing at a time. While he is working on the condor, that is all he will do. He will never play cello while he is working on condors." The cello never really came up again in our conversations.

The field teams were critical for keeping a consistent flow of information about where the birds were and what they were doing. Finding people who were rugged as well as bright and able to think on their feet was important. Sadly, field biologists were notorious for having too little interaction with civilized people, and our early condor field team was no exception. Rob Ramey was one of those, terribly smart with too little human interaction and a wicked sense of humor. On one particularly difficult hike with a heavily loaded pack, I was burning out way too early. Rob was behind me, ribbing me all the way. "What's the matter, Bill? Can't you handle the hills?" or "Do you need a push or someone to carry your pack?" Finally, Rob, in a rare show of sympathy, said, "Hey, why don't we all take a break and let Bill catch his breath? There's a stream just below. Let's get a cold drink." We all dropped our packs, in my case, very willingly. Rob then suggested that we didn't want to lose track of where we left our gear and said, "We should leave a line of breadcrumbs. You know, little rock piles every so often so we don't lose track of our stuff." Tired and sweaty, everyone looked around, and Noel announced he didn't see any rocks. Rob's beautifully timed reply came as he dug into my very heavy backpack."I know where some rocks are" All along our way in, Rob had been feeding rocks into my backpack. I have not gotten even with him, but I am not dead yet!

One of the more frustrating things about studying birds is that they get up so darn early. That is, most birds do; condors are a notable exception. It was an unintended stroke of good fortune that I could not study finches because, unlike finches, condors depend on sun-warmed updrafts—thermals—for flight. As a result, they sleep in, waiting for the day to heat up. This always gave me a little time after the early morning sun woke me to get organized and plan the day.

Everywhere condors went, we followed them. From Ventura County to Santa Barbara County to Los Angeles County, their travels led us by idyllic creeks and glens, open ranchland, and rugged chaparral-covered hills. I watched condors go to water; they were picky about their spots. On one particularly hot day, they found a quiet ravine, where the stream trickled down a rock-strewn gully and emptied into a quiet pool. I watched them cool off and decided I could learn something from them. Once they left, there seemed to be no reason for me to avoid the water. It created a lasting memory of the remarkably pristine places still to be found in California. Because of the condors, this area had the highest levels of protection. No one, not even biologists, was allowed into the area without official permits. I waded in the pool and could see trout swimming away. I was able to herd one into a corner and actually catch it by hand. That was dinner as I sat by a small campfire and watched a golden sun drop below the horizon.

As we had learned with the Andean condors, the California condor also typically laid one egg every two years, so there was no reproductive failure of any note. They were just naturally slow. They didn't build a nest; instead, they searched out a safe cave in the cliffs or on the hillsides to raise their single chick. Because they tended to be gorge feeders, they didn't need to find food every day. All these factors contributed to a relatively idyllic lifestyle for the condor and, as a result, for me. Condors relied as little as possible on flapping flight, preferring to let the wind and thermals do the hard work. Likely as not, it would be around nine or ten in the morning before the condors would leave their roosts and begin their day. Though I had to be in the observation blind before light, I could nap with confidence until the day warmed up.

Unlike the remarkably serene condors who lived their days unaware of the threats that faced them, the human portion of the program was emotionally and politically volatile. We were constantly embroiled in controversy, and it was often confusing because some of the biggest opposition to the recovery work was coming from the "conservation" community. There was money, emotions, reputations, and careers at stake. It was hard to know who your enemies might be and often harder still to be sure of your friends. It was not unusual for alliances to shift on one issue or the other, making it all the more complicated to know where things stood. Officially, only the Audubon Society, the state and federal government, and the San Diego and Los Angeles zoos were involved. But there was plenty of input from FOE, the Sierra Club, and the indigenous communities. In this explosive atmosphere, people came and went from the project literally overnight. Rarely did anyone leave willingly, and literally no one who left happily. Some people were, in a professional sense, murdered; their career ended by nasty politics. Early on, I decided I wanted to survive, and when the time came to leave the program, I was committed to departing by my own design. Fresh out of school, this soon-to-be classic program would be my professional baptism by fire.

I was mentored by Art Risser when I was at the zoo and Noel Snyder when I was in the field. On a daily basis, I found myself in the company of curious personalities and minds far greater than my own. Through all of this, I listened and absorbed an amazing amount of ornithological *and* political knowledge. These great intellects were great scientists but often unable or unwilling to "dumb down" their knowledge for the general public. Their biggest crime was that they wanted you to understand the details and the multiple outcomes that could result from any decision. Turned out, this was not what people wanted. People listening to the news had busy lives and wanted to know that you were proceeding with certainty and the outcome would be good. Scientists seemed unable to communicate that way. Media experts would tell you that most widely read periodicals were written at a ninth-grade reading level. We learned early that TV and newspapers had a hard time understanding and contextualizing the condor story. David Brower from Friends of the Earth was the master of the memorable sound bite, and no one on our side of the argument seemed to have the answer. I enjoyed the media and learned to play the interpreter for my more brilliant colleagues. In addition to my other responsibilities, it became my niche to be a spokesperson for the thoughts and ramblings of my fellow condor experts. Or, as Marcia Hobbs of the Los Angeles Zoo once bitterly opined, I became a "media hog."

This skill got me into important meetings, media events, conferences, Fish and Game Commission hearings, and more. While I could translate science into simple English, my eagerness to get it all out often neutered the message in formal debates outside of a press conference. Fortunately, I had Noel to teach me the arguments and Art to teach me timing and social finesse. I remember early on, in a particularly vicious and contentious Fish and Game Commission hearing, the three of us were sitting together while arguments and insults flew from the podium. Someone repeatedly abused Art Risser, asking him to identify himself and comment, but he didn't budge or let on that he was even there. It was not until all had been said and the meeting was near adjournment that Art finally introduced himself, clobbered our opponents with brilliant, thoughtful counterarguments, and closed the meeting. It was his words that would be left in everyone's minds as they left the meeting, and there was no rebuttal. His timing was perfect, his arguments polished, and his demeanor calm. He was elegant and educational. My future training included brutal kicks under the table and Art telling me when to speak and when to stop. I learned that timing combined with solid information created magic when well executed. I never forgot the lessons, but I am not sure I have ever fully mastered their delivery.

Chapter 10

The
PROMISE

"There's no abiding success without commitment."
-TONY ROBBINS

The first Andean condor I raised was Rodan, named after a famed Japanese daikaiju monster. He lived up to his name, topping out at about thirty-three pounds with an eleven-foot wingspan. Through most of the rearing process, condors were perhaps best described as the Labrador retriever of birds. Big, friendly, happy-go-lucky, and lovable. This was a source of both good and bad news. Friendly to a fault, Andean condors were unafraid of people, and many times, the various vulture chicks I was working with would flop down on my feet as I sat at my desk. They loved the attention and mutual grooming with me, but these behaviors would not do them well if they were released into the wild. Should the day come when we would raise a California condor, that bird

Getting Rodan into the net wasn't the point; the point rather was to spook him enough that he'd regurgitate, providing me with proper (if slightly gross) food for the baby vultures.

would have to be fit enough to return to the wild, and that meant it could not want to associate with people.

When it came to this type of bonding, we were dealing with a behavioral issue known as imprinting. It was here that my early fascination with Konrad Lorenz would pay off. Considered to be the father of the science of ethology, the study of animal behavior under natural conditions, he coined the word imprinting to describe a developmentally sensitive phase that allowed for an irreversible form of learning. Basically, the kind of

We recognized early the power of the media, so a few birds like this female Andean condor were habituated to people and the camera.

imprinting we were concerned with in condors was filial imprinting, the brief moment in life when a baby bird identified its cohorts, birds of the same species. Lorenz defined the behavior in geese, but it was pretty ubiquitous in birds. The challenge ahead of us as we tried rearing condor chicks was not simply to hatch an egg and have the baby survive, but to carefully manage this learning so that they wouldn't be confused and think of humans as parents, friends, or mates. There was a very long history of handmade, birdlike models being used to raise baby birds, especially in falconry, but it took the creative mind of Art Risser to take it to the next level of lifelike, functional arm puppets that could feed, groom, and even discipline the young condor chicks. By operating these puppets from behind an opaque blind, the idea was that the condor would never see a person, only another condor to develop a relationship with.

Back at the zoo, I reared Andean condors and worked with San Diego's Puppet Ladies, Marie Hitchcock and Genevieve Engman, to refine the design and function of the lifelike arm puppets we would use to feed the chicks.

Marie Hitchcock and I with her first Andean condor
puppet created for feeding our babies.

Handling both adult and baby Andean condors at the zoo placed me in a unique position with the recovery team. I was the only person who regularly handled condors. So when disaster struck in 1980, when a wild California condor chick died while being handled and measured in the field, my name came up. The program was made up of biologists, and the academic curriculum for biology was painfully lacking when it came to actually working with live animals. Academia could be an isolated and theoretical world, and in this case, it was fatal for a young condor. As dedicated a team as it was, they missed numerous signs of stress, and the chick collapsed and died in their hands. Instantly, any permits that allowed for the handling of birds evaporated, and the program was thrown into turmoil. One result of that fiasco was the determination that in the future, professional animal handlers from either the San Diego Zoo or the Los Angeles Zoo would have to be present whenever a wild condor was handled. Again, chance placed me in a remarkable position; as San Diego's only condor keeper, I and/or one of the zoo veterinarians had to be present for all early interactions with condors.

Some of the first real dramas under the new rules played out in 1982. The male parent of a half-grown condor chick failed to come and feed the chick. At first, we were unconcerned, but after a day or two, it was clear something was terribly wrong, and this young chick would soon starve to death if no action was taken to save it. The program applied for an emergency permit. Phil Ensley, a zoo veterinarian, and I went to stay at Noel's home in Ojai near the condor sanctuary to prepare for the rescue. Our departure from Noel's home would have to be in the very early morning. Members of the team would fly by helicopter to an area near the site, and the chick would be rescued and brought to San Diego for care. Midway into the fast-moving operation, a radio call informed us that several conservation groups had raised objections. A federal judge determined that our work should be suspended until the issues could be settled. At this point, the chick's survival was on the line. Days of discussion in Washington would be deadly. If a death occurred because of this indecision, it would not be death by starvation, but death by politics.

We returned to Noel's home, where he launched into a long day of phone calls and pleas that ultimately ended with permission to rescue the chick. It was too late in the day to mobilize again, so we went to bed early to be ready for another predawn journey into the mountains.

In the darkness, we gathered our gear and headed to the field. This time, there was no last-minute radio call, and the rescue proceeded without a hitch. As the helicopter headed for San Diego with its precious cargo, a handful of us stood happily on the roadway, reliving the exciting moments of the morning. Finding some perverse pleasure in the politics, I commented on how lucky we were not to have received another radio call that would have ended the rescue. Noel's face lit up as he informed our small group he wasn't sure if we had gotten a call or not. He had intentionally left the radio at home.

Later, out of respect for the Chumash tribe and the Great Spirit, this rescued chick was named Xolxol. He thrived in his new setting and began to reveal the true hardiness of the California condor. His first meal made headlines across most of the US and gave us a shot at some positive publicity. He grew rapidly and left the nest on schedule, all without incident. Finally, a bird had been handled and transported successfully. The program had its first new chick

Nothing could bring a smile to Noel's face like knowing he had done the right thing at the right time and ensured another condor would survive.

on which to begin building a captive population. Retrospectively, we believe the male condor may have been sick, most likely from lead poisoning and then recovered because several weeks later he showed up again. Most importantly, he went on to father chicks the following year. Much of the delay and hyperbole in the program was based on Carl Koford's landmark book, *The California Condor,* where he allowed his desire to protect the condors to affect what he wrote about them. One of the erroneous takeaways from this iconic book was that if you entered a breeding pair's habitat, they would break up and never breed again. We had finally and definitively shown that Carl Koford, Audubon's condor man, had indeed misled the world.

The ideal scenario was to build a safe, genetically sound captive population without detrimental impact on the wild population. K.C. Lint had clearly demonstrated with Andean condors that removing an egg from their nest would prompt them to "recycle" and lay a replacement egg. The team saw the opportunity to collect an egg for the zoos with confidence that the birds would lay another egg, raise a chick, and all would be the same for the wild birds. The success with Xolxol made it possible for Noel and the team to plan for the collection of a viable condor egg.

The following year, Dr. Noel Snyder and I climbed into a condor nest and took their egg.

Noel and I prepared and rehearsed endlessly for the moment when we'd collect that egg. We practiced maintaining a safe transport temperature in a specially designed case by adding hot water bottles at appropriate intervals. Climbers rigged ropes up a rocky cliff and pitched a tent just out of view of the condor nest. Neither Noel nor I was eager to find ourselves in high places or had any experience on ropes. We waited to climb to our suspended tent until it was dark. In my mind, we went at night so that I would not have to look down while we were climbing. There was also hope that this would mask our activities from the birds.

The plan was to remain in the tent, monitoring our radio. We could not see the opening to the nest from where we were stationed, so an observer watching from nearly a mile away would call us when the bird incubating the egg got up to leave the nest. We did not want to flush or frighten the bird from the nest for fear that in his or her haste to get away from us the egg might get damaged or, worse yet, kicked out of the cave and down the cliff.

Our patience would now be tried against the patience of a vulture. Like the old cowboy movies where mute vultures were voiced over with screams of a red-tailed hawk as they perched endlessly waiting patiently for something or someone to die, the bird on the egg had this kind of patience.

Noel and I went through a ritual that was repeated multiple times a day. We would heat water to a precise temperature and pour it into hot water bottles. These bottles were placed in an insulated case with a special hollow to receive the egg. The box was closed and carefully brought to temperature. From repeated experiments at Noel's home, we knew what temperature to keep the hot water bottles at in order to bring the box back to temperature as the bottles in the box cooled. It was a constant cycle of keeping properly heated hot water bottles on hand and cycling them through the egg box.

The first day came, and we heated our bottles, quietly sang the lyrics from our musical hero Randy Newman, and talked about condors, the politics, and the uncertain future of our work and our lives. As the sun set, lizards headed for cracks in the rocks to huddle away for the night. We prepped our simple meals and got a long night's rest. The cycle repeated itself on day two: heating water, growing weary of Randy Newman, watching lizards and birds, and waiting. Nearly a mile away from us, an observer was going through a similar day. Their powerful scope directed into the nest cave, watching every move the bird made and reporting to us as time crept by.

The original plan had been to wait for a call from the observers announcing that the bird was off the egg. But the weather was dynamic, nice at one moment and rainy the next. We were concerned the bird might move away from the egg at a time when the weather was too bad to get a helicopter in to us. Finally, after several days, we decided to make the move. We would approach the nest slowly, talking loudly as we went to announce our presence without it being a surprise. As we drew closer, the bird stood and moved to the opening of the cave. Noel and I picked up our volume and our pace to prevent the bird from returning to the nest. We were too hyped on the adrenaline of the moment to be too afraid of the amazing height we were at, but we were careful. We could not afford to have an accident of any type now that we were in motion. As we approached the cave, the mother condor watched us with concern but hesitantly left the nest and took flight.

Only moments later, we found ourselves sitting inside a cave in the rugged mountains of Ventura County. We were in the cave, squatting on either side of the egg, resting alone on the gravel floor.

In my mind, I could imagine the tiny embryo in this egg and how our actions would change its life. I remember it as a moment of necessity, but also profound sadness.

Noel and I had planned every detail, every step, every movement. We checked the temperature in the egg box and examined and photographed the egg to document any damage prior to our touching it. Every few moments, the condor flew by the opening of the cave, obviously distressed that her home had been invaded and protective of her valuable egg. With each pass she made, the interior of the cave darkened as her huge wingspan blocked the sun. We were invading her most personal space and taking her egg, her future. I remembered my thrill and feelings of the first condor I had seen a few years earlier. That moment had been so magical and, for lack of a better term, so equal—neither of us was in charge of the other. This was tragically different. I welled up with a suffocating sense of sadness and regret. If there was a tiny viable embryo in this egg, and the chick hatched successfully at the zoo, it would never fly free according to the recovery plan. There would be no high-altitude climbs lifted by warm thermals, no graceful falls into a hundred-mile glide, no frolicking in the streams, no sunning on the cliffs. This bird would live the rest of its life in captivity, in a cage forty feet wide, eighty feet long, and twenty feet high. The immensity of what we were doing did not escape either of us. At that moment, I made a promise to the tiny embryo and to the condors as a species to stay until the balance was reset or all was lost. I would have no career choices until a California condor was released into the wild to balance this act. In reality, I had no idea what I had just committed myself to do, but it was a commitment I would see through one way or another.

There was a pause before the egg was moved because one step had not been planned. Noel looked at me and said something along the lines of, "From here on, it is your responsibility. You pick it up." And so it was with gloved hands, I lifted this precious egg from the nest and into the box. From there, it was a long, cautious process to get ourselves and our valuable cargo off the cliff and up the mountain to the rough pad where the helicopter would meet us and carry us to San Diego. The box with the egg was never in our hands if we were moving. I would move past Noel, and he would hand me the box, then Noel would move past me, and I would hand him the box.

We finally arrived at a pre-cleared pad, where a helicopter collected Noel and me, and we were off to the San Diego Zoo's parking lot.

There would be other egg-pick trips that year, three more in fact, and our technique of approaching the nest in conversation became a protocol. One trip stood out as a story of Noel's determination. Our team was flown to within about a mile of a nest site and dropped off. From there, we hiked to our camp and prepared to collect the egg, hopefully, the following day if all went well. At the campsite, we settled in. Noel checked in via his Fish and Wildlife Service radio. When he was done, I knew immediately something was wrong. Apparently, there was a storm headed our way. If it stayed on course, they would be unable to get a helicopter to us if we picked up the egg. That meant everything was going to be put on hold for a few days. Noel's biggest fear throughout the program was lost time. He did not want to be stuck in the field, unable to do any work. A request was sent for the helicopter to return, but the pilot declined, citing inclement weather. Not to be thwarted, Noel decided if we left soon and traveled light, we could make it to the outskirts of Ojai, where Helen could pick us up by nightfall. We packed away our gear, grabbed some water, and set out at a fast pace through the dry chaparral. It was a butt-breaking walk, but at least we were not burdened with gear. Just as the sun set, Helen picked up a few tired biologists and drove them home.

Noel stayed right on top of the news and, at some point during the evening, learned that the most violent part of the storm would slide by without hitting us. Not wanting to waste time, another call went to the pilot, requesting a helicopter. We were turned down again because of the weather. The decision was made that, minus all our gear, we could hike back to the nest site in the morning and make our egg pick up the following day. And so, with me complaining the whole time, we left in the dark, predawn hours and started our trek back to the nest site. Probably more than halfway into our trek, the bad weather hit: heavy fog, drizzle, and occasional light snow. We literally could not see where we were going and had no gear with us to prepare for a night in the snow.

We (Noel) made a classically bad decision. We would keep the rise of the mountain to our left and continue on until we could get our bearings. This turned out to be a bad idea. After several hours of difficult hiking, we came across our own footprints in the mud. We had circled the top of the mountain and made absolutely no progress. It was getting dark. It was cold and wet, and we had no gear and no idea where we were.

We took a break and assessed our situation. At the moment, there was no going forward and no going back. We were done moving for the night and decided we had to find or make shelter and fast. The landscape was spotted with huge granite boulders that pretty much all looked alike, but Noel was sure they were familiar and that there was a food stash nearby. I don't recall finding any food, but we found shelter in low caves under some boulders. Just outside the cave, we lit a fire for

That moment of realization—we are lost, and it is going to be a very cold night.

warmth. It turned out to be a long, cold night, and suffice it to say, I burned the soles off my shoes trying to stay warm and smacked my head more times than I cared to count trying to sit up in the cave.

When dawn finally came, carrying the biting cold that went with a clear sky, we were able to get our bearings and successfully complete our task.

Chapter 11

DEAD BIRDS,
Messy
POLITICS

"Try to interact with people who have a different political
perspective than you do—and when you do, listen to
understand, not just to refute."
~PETER WEHNER

In 1983, a very pregnant Cyndi Kuehler led the team in hatching
that first egg and producing the first chick hatched in captivity—Sisquoc. The media's reaction to Sisquoc was swift and quite
overwhelming. For Cyndi, who was an introvert, she could imagine
nothing worse. This would be the beginning of her own personal
war against the media that would continue until they no longer
cared to speak with her. We received a call in the incubation room

from Art Risser, requesting our presence for a press conference. I responded I would be right down, but Art said to wait. He would send a security car to escort me down. That seemed odd, but okay by me because it was a bit of a walk to the administration building. The station wagon arrived and off we went. When we arrived, I knew something was different. Security was everywhere. I was escorted into a large room called the Rondavel, where I was met by Art, Noel, and a battery of cameras and microphones like I had never seen. Either trapped in the mountains of Southern California or locked in the incubation room for weeks on end, I was out of the loop when it came to the media's interest in what we were doing. In addition, I don't think anyone in the program expected the media event that occurred because of this little chick.

The hatching of Sisquoc instantly changed the tenor of the program. With the media and global community cheering, the naysayers were largely silenced.

We received congratulatory calls from the White House, Prince Charles, and more. With the hatching of Sisquoc, we had captured the attention of the world. It was not so much that we had silenced our adversaries, as it was that people no longer wanted to hear what they had to say. The voice of the team, and specifically the Zoological

Society of San Diego, had become the voice for the condor. Politically, the tide had turned in favor of the program and, more importantly, in favor of the condor, and would remain so for the rest of the time I spent with the program.

For Cyndi and me personally, the next big event in our lives would be the birth of our daughter, Emily. Despite our fancy Mexican divorce, someone in the media learned that the lady hatching the condors was pregnant and that the father of her baby was also the person raising the baby condors. Things got dicey very quickly; everyone in the media wanted to do a story on the condor couple who were having a baby. Cyndi and I knew that sooner or later, someone would find out we were not married. For the very conservative Zoological Society of San Diego, a high-profile baby being born out of wedlock under the eyes of local media was an embarrassment—especially if it was discovered that it was their policies that forced a divorce and illicit sex acts that led to a child. Much to our amusement, someone from the zoo's board of trustees contacted us at the hospital. The first sentence was, "Congratulations on all your success. We have changed our employment policies, and we want you to get married again." The second sentence was, "Can we send a press contingent to the hospital to do a story about your baby?" So much for the nepotism rule. For all the loving couples that followed us at the Zoological Society of San Diego, you are welcome.

For the first time in decades, the condor program was enveloped in good news. On the zoo end of things, the stream of good news seemed endless as, year after year, more babies were successfully hatched and reared. Without the throb of good news from the zoos, I am not certain the condor program would have had the public support necessary to overcome the next extraordinarily tragic obstacles.

The winter of 1984/85 was devastating to the condor population. Birds seemed to simply evaporate. It rapidly became clear that we were down to one breeding pair of condors and some singles in the wild. It was in moments like this that fragile alliances were tested, and that was what happened. Birds had done well in captivity, eggs hatched with great regularity, and disasters in the zoos, as opposed to the field, were pretty much nonexistent. Prior to the collapse of the wild population, the excitement among recovery team members was such that there had been many discussions about releasing birds back into the wild well ahead of schedule, but the disappearance of so many birds in such a short window of time changed that discussion for most members of the recovery team. For some, this tragic winter die-off meant we should hurry and release birds to supplement the crashing population. For most of the others, it was an indication that we could not protect the birds in the wild, and we would be risking everything to return birds to the wild prematurely.

By the spring of 1986, none of the birds that had disappeared during the winter of 1985 had re-appeared. It became abundantly clear to many of us in the program that we were not going to be able to save the wild population of California condors. It was no surprise that this revelation would be controversial news, especially coming as it was, blanketed in nearly four years of positive news about population growth in the zoos. This was confusing to the media and, therefore, to just about everyone involved in influencing our permits. The recovery team, as often happens, was slowly becoming more and more political. We knew proposing the extirpation of the wild population would be a difficult decision to make by committee. A handful of us collaborated with Noel Snyder on a letter that was quickly known as the Valentine's Day Docufesto—or even worse, by some as the Bloody Valentine's Day Docufesto. Distributed on February 14, 1986, it both followed and led to great turmoil. This document called for all California condors to be brought into captivity as a last-ditch effort to protect what little genetic diversity was left in a failing population. There had, of course, been detailed conversations about what it would mean to remove condors from the wild, but this was the first time that a full strategy was formally put forward on paper.

There were two big obstacles to implementing the strategies laid out in the Valentine's Day document. One of them would play out publicly in court, and the other would be largely managed quietly and a great deal more civilly. The one that played out in the courts was the obstruction by the National Audubon Society, and the other was the resistance by the Native Americans, specifically the Chumash. The Chumash had watched our work carefully and with a certain degree of cynicism over the years, but this was a crisis. Our proposal meant they would most certainly lose their connection to the spirit world.

While Art and I would file amicus briefs with the courts on behalf of the San Diego Zoological Society, the untimely deaths of condors would ultimately influence the legal battles. More intimately, I would have partial responsibility for negotiating with the Chumash elders. Numerous meetings were held with the Chumash elders, but little progress was made. Specifically, their concern was that without condors in the wild, they would be deprived of their route to the spirit world. The condor enclosures, popularly called the condorminiums, were a strict no-visit zone at the San Diego Wild Animal Park. Only specific keepers and park veterinarians were permitted at the facility. There had been rants from the Friends of the Earth that condors would be better off dead than in captivity. As a result, their enclosures were surrounded by an eight-foot chain-link fence with razor wire looped around the top. Among the requests being made by the Chumash was to be allowed to visit the facilities and bless the condors.

After a brief internal discussion, I suggested we agree to have them visit the Wild Animal Park for a meeting, but not the condor facility. I was told they would not show up or would be late and that either way, it was likely that no good would come of the visit. It was finally agreed that it would do no harm to set a meeting.

They wanted to come on a weekend, which was going to be a challenge for me, but the meeting was set. The flamboyant divorce papers

Cyndi and I had purchased in Mexico had evolved into a far less impressive reality as we parted ways as amicably as we could. By now, we had our second child, David, and I had moved out of the house. On many occasions, caring for the kids on weekends became a weapon in our eroding relationship rather than an opportunity. We were both guilty. In this case, it was my weekend with Emily and David, and there was no way Cyndi would cover for me. Too proud to ask for help from my family, I decided the kids would just have to come to the meeting with the elders.

It was a warm, late summer day, and not only did the Chumash keep their appointment, but there were more of them than I was expecting. Several of them brought their kids. While we held our preliminary meeting on the edge of the lagoon in the public area of the park, our kids got to know each other in a way that often fails adults. The kids had a common interest, their fascination with animals, water, and the desire to play. While the elders and I tried to

The Chumash people taught me a lot about the value of respect for the beliefs of others and the progress that could be made when people treat one another like family.

understand our complicated positions, our children did their own form of team building and played their hearts out.

We discussed serious issues of life, the afterlife, and being good parents. We kept an eye on our children as they played, catching each other's eyes at those moments that would touch our hearts or make us laugh. The warmth that came naturally for our children warmed our hearts and helped us define our own common passions: our love for our children and their future. This was a lesson that greatly informed my career in conservation.

It was in that common and genial atmosphere I decided to break the rules and allow them to visit the condor breeding area. We would remain outside the chain-link fence. It was agreed that the elders could perform a ceremony to bless the condors. From the gravel driveway outside the security fence, we could see the condors on their perches, their wings open to the last rays of the fading sun. The elders squatted in the gravel, drew a large circle, and spread tobacco. They formed a circle and began to slowly move and quietly chant. Music and the rhythms of our hearts were contagious, but I knew this was not my celebration. I stood back at a respectful distance to watch, holding my kids close to me. David and Emily were not yet wise enough to understand that this was not their ceremony, and, caught up in the chanting, they slipped away and danced their way towards the circle. Embarrassed and in a bit of a panic, I started to rush forward to corral my ignorant and overeager offspring, but before I could get there, hands reached out from the circle and pulled them in. Now it was inclusive, our ceremony of a common dream built on our love of family. It was a blessing for all, and the Chumash agreed to the path forward to save the condors. Wisdom sometimes comes in very small packages.

Chapter 12

Extirpation,
EMPTY SKIES

"It's so much darker when a light goes out than it would
have been if it had never shone."
-JOHN STEINBECK

That left one more hurdle, and that was the near-constant
resistance by the National Audubon Society. Though it was a
federally led program, the US Fish and Wildlife Service could not
lobby for their own budget—that work was done by the National
Audubon Society, and it left them with an enormous amount of
leverage over the program. I often wondered why such a respected
conservation organization was so frequently on the wrong side of
progress in the condor's recovery. I believed the challenge for all
of us was to look at the big picture and somehow leave out the
consideration of how any particular decision might affect me as
opposed to the impact on the condors. Day by day, it was painful
for me to have taken an egg from the wild and see these spectacular

birds in cages, but it was always the big picture that made it marginally tolerable. For the Chumash, the short-term picture was the challenge of getting into the spirit world without condors in the wild. Knowing that no action might mean extinction, where their path to the spirit world would be permanently erased, helped them accept short-term discomfort. I had trouble understanding why the Audubon Society lacked this vision. It turned out I needed to understand the organization's short-term pain in order to shed some light on their behavior. One day, the light came on. There were three consequences the Audubon Society wanted to avoid. First, they had long been lobbying to acquire the Hudson Ranch, and wild birds and Audubons involvement was key to that. Second, the condor was a money-making machine for them, but only as long as they were wild. Third, it provided employment for their team. I think their position had very little to do with saving the condor and more with pumping up their bank accounts and keeping their team employed. The same kinds of pressures could also apply to zoos. Condors had huge donor appeal, and it was exploited as fully as possible, but under the unique and balanced leadership of Art Risser in San Diego, the good of the condor always came first.

The huge wintertime loss of 60% of the population made us all hyper-vigilant. The response of the federal government was to forbid the recovery team from holding meetings. I suppose the intent was to make political decisions from the top. The members of the recovery team knew how to contact each other, so there were constant unofficial meetings and phone calls as we tried to pave the way to bring the last birds into protective custody. As the political and legal battles raged on, our field crews were doing all they could to protect the vulnerable wild birds. It was protocol to capture radio-tagged birds on a set schedule to check the batteries in the tags and take blood samples so we could monitor for lead poisoning. A condor dubbed SBF was held up by Audubon Society biologists as *the* bird that was using safe provisions (food known to be lead free) and was therefore very safe and should be left in the wild. She was briefly captured for a radio tag replacement, a blood sample was taken and she was released. When her samples came back, it was discovered that her blood lead levels were dangerously elevated. Treating lead poisoning if caught early enough was generally a straightforward process of using a chelating agent to remove lead from the bloodstream. Part of Audubon's failing argument was that they could protect wild birds by providing them with clean (lead-free) carcasses, and this bird, they felt, could be better protected than any of the others. As the Audubon Society filed a federal lawsuit to obtain an injunction against bringing the last condors into captivity, an ailing SBF lost her ability to fly and was picked up and brought to the San Diego

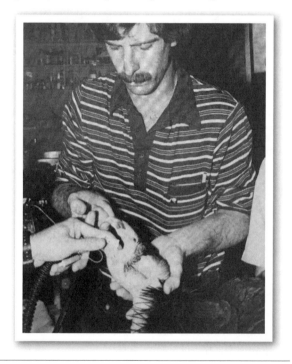

Critics of the program often told us to allow the condors to die in peace.
There's nothing peaceful about a slow and painful death from lead
poisoning, nor in the knowledge that it was we humans who caused it.

Wild Animal Park. Despite round-the-clock heroic efforts to save her, on January 18, 1986, she died and, with her, the viability of the Audubon Society's lawsuit.

The condor program was a huge doorway to opportunity. My name was suddenly known in the conservation world. So many people who I had looked up to for so long now saw me as a colleague. I had wonderful correspondence with Konrad Lorenz, my long-time hero and guru of animal behavior. Among those who I was honored to know was the zoo's goodwill ambassador, Joan Embery. Along with many other amazing credentials, she was the most frequent zoo guest of *The Tonight Show* with Johnny Carson, and with all those visits, she and the show's team had a great relationship. So one day, Johnny Carson and his wife Alexis Maas were going to visit the Wild Animal Park with Joan Embery as their host. Sadly for Joan, she was ill that day. She called me and asked if I could stand in for her and take Johnny out for the day. I was excited both about seeing Johnny again and the fact that I always enjoyed getting to drive around in the field exhibits—it never seemed to grow old. True to Dr. Charles Schroeder's dream for this park, several of the exhibits were more than one hundred acres in size and filled with herds of animals from East Africa. It meant we could go on a bumpy truck ride pretty close to a real East African safari.

We warmed up to each other quickly and settled into our safari. Shortly before lunch, we came across a giraffe who was in labor. I described in some detail the mechanics of a giraffe birth, which takes place with the mother standing. It was a long drop to the ground, and that sudden stop at the end helped clear the newborn's airways in the same way that spanking a baby's bottom might get things going. They inquired as to how long this labor might last. I really didn't have any idea, but Johnny said they were not in a hurry, which meant I wasn't either. We parked the truck, lunch was brought out to us, and we told each other jokes. Sometimes all three of us were laughing so hard we couldn't speak. I felt like I had connected in a special way with a truly remarkable man. For me, it was a pretty memorable day.

Apparently, Johnny Carson felt at least a little bit the same. It was only a few days after his visit when the phone rang. It was someone from *The Tonight Show* telling me that Johnny had requested I come be a guest on his show. So on May 11, 1988, I sat beside Johnny on the set of *The Tonight Show*. We retold stories of the giraffe's birth, filled a curious nation in on the state of the condor program, and I was left with an enduring memory of an interesting man I am honored to have met.

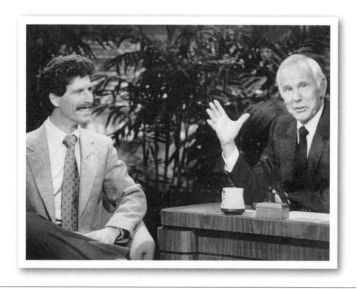

Johnny Carson, the iconic talk show host, was a lesson in composure and had a true connection and natural ability with animals.

Chapter 13

RETURN
of the
CONDOR

"Success is simple.
Do what's right, the right way, at the right time."
~ARNOLD H. GLASOW

The rapid-fire successes of the condor program had made me a bit giddy and feeling unbeatable. While I was still a condor keeper, I got into an enormous policy battle that was way above my paygrade with the manager at the Wild Animal Park. Shortly after our battle, he was promoted to executive director of the Zoological Society. It was only shortly after his promotion that the position of assistant curator of birds opened up, a position that would ultimately have to be approved by the new director. I applied and interviewed for the job. Nothing happened. I was not hired, but neither was anyone else. Finally, after weeks of pins and needles, Art Risser came to me and said he had selected me, but the executive director was blocking it. An honorable man, Art Risser had held out for what he felt was best for the organization, but now it was up to me to do something to fix my damaged relationship with the director. I had to swallow my pride, humble myself, and apologize to the director and describe how I would perform differently in the position of assistant curator. It was a great lesson the director did not make easy—he canceled several appointments at the last minute. Finally, I was allowed to see him, apologize, and plead my case.

A few tense days went by before I was called in to see Art and was awarded the position. I was only in my late twenties, and this was the achievement of a childhood dream and a moment of incredible elation. Like the curators before me, I was determined that THIS was the job I would one day retire from after many successful decades. With my role in the condor program winding down, I could really learn what this special job was all about.

Most of my graduate school had been spent trying to capture and collect samples from turkey vultures. My time at the zoo had thus far been all about the California condor. I was pretty much the only one around with a specialty in vultures, so leaving it completely behind would take time. It was okay. I rather enjoyed being the odd man out, or the only one "outstanding" in my field.

Earlier I mentioned the spaghetti westerns with vultures circling over dead and dying cowboys; now it was my turn to get some first-hand experience. It started with a phone call from an attorney who then had me talk to a detective. The story I was told took place in Trinity County, a county in the northwestern part of California. It was a rugged backwater community known as Hawkins Bar. There was a general store, a BP gas station, and a bar. Apparently, a local resident had gone out looking for firewood and noticed turkey vultures circling low in the air. Guessing the birds had found something to eat, he went to explore. What he discovered was the partially buried body of Mr. Gary Summar. Mr. Summar had been dead for several days and, in addition to being the victim of a brutal murder, had been food for carrion eaters. Mr. Summar had most likely been wrongly accused of raping a young relative of a friend. True or not, the locals decided to take the law into their own hands. They took Mr. Summar out and beat him with their fists and a baseball bat, stabbed him more than seventy times, and finally, ran him over with a pickup truck. With that punishment completed, he was dumped into a shallow grave. I remember clearly the laugh that came from the detective when he wrapped up the description of the murder by saying, "Worse case of suicide I have ever seen."

After the body was discovered, the story rapidly unfolded, and nine people, mostly from one family, were arrested and charged with murder. I came into the story at the penalty phase of the trial. The father was accused of taking a "trophy," Mr. Summar's ear, and showing it off in a local bar. If that was proven to be the case, it would be considered special circumstances in the State of California, and he would be eligible for the death penalty. This was where I came in. Without going into the gory details, I had to examine photos of the body taken by detectives at the gravesite. They knew animals had gotten to the body, so the question put to me was, "Which missing parts were eaten by animals and which parts might have been cut off by the killers?"

While there was clearly the chance that other vermin had gotten to the body, it was fairly clear from droppings and feathers that turkey vultures had spent a lot of time with Mr. Summar's body. American vultures are not powerful birds. They have extremely weak feet and a strong but not particularly sharp beak. When feeding on carrion, they feed at soft access points first: eyes, ears, mouth, rectum, etc. So, it was no surprise to me that the dead man's lips, eyes, and most importantly, his exposed ear would be missing, but it left unanswered the challenge of determining by whose hand or beak the ear in question was taken.

The giveaway was in a photograph taken before the man was murdered. In that photograph, he wore an earring in the ear that later went missing. I knew from chasing vultures around cattle and sheep ranches that vultures did not like hard objects like ear tags. Ranchers often used these to identify their animals, and when a vulture would find one of them dead, they would pull the tag out and drop it before feeding on the ear. At my request, detectives returned to the gravesite, sifted the soil, and lo and behold, found Gary Summar's earring.

Now I had to convince the court. I decided a nice video would help illustrate my case. I purchased an earring similar to the one the man had in his ear, put that earring into the ear of a dead rabbit, and filmed it as turkey vultures went to feed on it. They did as I expected. They pulled the earring out and dropped it into the dirt before consuming the ear. With video in hand, I was ready for my day in court, or so I thought. I grew up in the country, and hauling around dead calves, goats, and sheep for vulture bait somehow seemed like a logical extension of my youth. For dress, I had no recollection of ever owning anything other than hiking boots, Levi's, and plaid shirts. The defense attorney called to interview me prior to our court date. At the end of the discussion, I was told it would be a good idea to wear a suit to court. Good idea? It didn't seem like it, but they were going to pay me for my testimony, so it was off to the clothing store.

I had never buttoned my collar before. I had no idea whatsoever that some shirts could be purchased with different-sized collars. Who knew? I had a pretty tough time buttoning the shirt, but I managed. I put on a cheap tie and dress shoes, figured I was good to go, and headed off to court. The whole thing was a little nerve-wracking. I was called to the stand to testify. I'm not sure of the exact physiology that went on when I nervously took the stand, but it seemed like my neck must have swelled up. They asked a question, and I simply could not speak. Not one word would come out past my tie and tightly buttoned collar. Fearing that I would die on the stand, I quickly loosened my tie, undid that top button, and successfully continued with my testimony. Our client successfully avoided the death penalty, and I went off to buy some new shirts.

The days in my new job were busy. The focus was intense, and some things suffered. Years in the program were wearing on me. I had gotten a divorce, and my work had become much more administrative and political, but I continued to serve on the recovery team. I was still fully committed to seeing the program go full circle, to see a condor fly free while I was still partly responsible.

Ten years after bringing the rescued chick Xolxol into captivity, nine years after collecting the egg that had produced Sisquoc, and several years of active service on the federally-appointed California Condor Recovery Team, I was there to finally close the circle. I was there to witness the first release of two California condors back into the wild.

It was January 15, 1992, and biologists and journalists had come from all over the world to the Sespe Condor Sanctuary. This was very odd. Sanctuary was a legal term for protected land in the United States. It was the highest level of protection that could be given to an area to protect a species. No one went into a sanctuary legally unless they had specific permits to do so. Through nearly a decade of access, I had become used to being in a wilderness area where I was most often truly alone. On this morning, in the wee hours before the sun rose, I looked down the mountain at a literal freeway of headlights on oil roads surrounding the sanctuary. Everyone seemed to be coming to be part of this moment. It will stick with me forever as contradictory but moving. The tide seemed finally to have truly turned in the condors' favor.

Armed with huge lenses, the media watched from a distance as two California condors were given their freedom. Seemingly hundreds of media cameras were focused on the release site, waiting for that moment when a condor would take to the sky and be free again. For most people, I think it was a bit anticlimactic. The birds stepped from the crates, walked onto a huge, grey granite boulder high in the mountains, rousted their feathers, and laid down in the sun. Countless news agencies and cameramen were disappointed. There was no dramatic launch of this amazing bird back into the skies of its home. But privately and quietly, I could not help but smile. For the first time in ten years, a California condor was free to do whatever it chose to do. Doing nothing was its choice, and that choice was good. I watched for a moment, pulled my letter of resignation from my pocket, handed it off to Lloyd Kiff, the recovery team leader, and with nothing else to do, turned around and walked away.

The condor program was never without drama. It seemed like nobody did what I did—came into the program, worked hard for several years, and then left under my own power with relatively few political scars. I was proud of that accomplishment, but it would be short-lived. I was asked by the regional director of the US Fish and Wildlife Service if I would please extend my tenure until we finished a re-drafted and updated recovery plan. Foolishly, I agreed.

The Peregrine Fund—an NGO established to recover the endangered peregrine falcon—was running out of work. With the banning of DDT in 1972, the biggest threat to the recovery of the peregrine was eliminated. While the Peregrine Fund did great work and garnered huge amounts of publicity, it was entirely likely that with the banning of DDT, the falcon would have recovered without the assistance of the Peregrine Fund. The organization recognized this and, with the falcon now thriving, was looking for another lifeline. The California condor seemed like a good one.

To the American public, this would all seem quite rational: the sight of two impressive birds of prey in trouble and the great reputation of the Peregrine Fund appeared on the surface to be a great match. To a condor biologist, knowing that the birds were not even distantly related and had no similarities in behavior or environmental challenges, the match was not quite so obvious.

In our first year of collecting condor eggs from the wild, we had collected four eggs. Each of the pairs laid a replacement egg, and all four of the eggs we collected hatched. All four of the chicks we hatched thrived. At the end of the season, Dr. Tom Cade, a professor and founder of the Peregrine Fund, sent a letter to the USFWS telling them they could have done it better. That did not sit well with many of us in the program, as we were batting a thousand. For my entire period in the program, there were five partners: the US Fish and Wildlife Service, the California Department of Fish and Game, the National Audubon Society (depending on their mood), and the two zoos, Los Angeles and San Diego. All the organizations had made enormous investments in the program, and in the case of the two zoos, with no support from the state or federal government.

By the time we released those first birds, the exploding population of captive condors made it clear other collaborators were going to be needed. The recovery team set out certain standards for what a new collaborator would have to provide. One of those things was that they, like the zoos, would have to provide their own funding. The logic was simple. Federal and state money should go to the bird's habitat and to implementing and enforcing whatever regulations would make that habitat a safer place for them to thrive. Anything that bled money from that aspect of the program was very much the enemy.

Our team leader, Lloyd Kiff, much like the Peregrine Fund, was looking for his next professional step and was quietly offered a position with the Peregrine Fund. To this day, I think this colored his thinking. It came as some surprise when I learned a bill was proceeding through Congress with millions of dollars of support for the Peregrine Fund to build captive breeding facilities for condors. I had an enormous but fruitless argument with Lloyd and other somewhat less committed members of the team. When that turned out to be a waste of time, I brought to bear whatever pressure I could through the San Diego Zoo and any other sympathetic group I could appeal to apply pressure on our legislators to stop this funding. In the end, I succeeded, and the funds were pulled from the bill. A very short time later, I received an angry call from the director of the Fish and Wildlife Service, which was quickly followed by a very nice letter from our regional director, thanking me for my time on the recovery team.

Lloyd left the recovery team in 1993 and joined the Peregrine Fund in 1994. Noel Snyder had long before been terminated by the USFWS for standing up for what he believed in and was playing his cello in Arizona. My time was done as well. It was time for me to really turn around and walk away.

United States Department of the Interior
FISH AND WILDLIFE SERVICE

911 N.E. 11th Avenue
Portland, Oregon 97232-4181

NOV 05 1992

Mr. William D. Toone
Curator of Birds
San Diego Wild Animal Park
15500 San Pasqual Valley Road
Escondido, California 92027-9614

Dear Mr. Toone:

We have received your letter to Lloyd Kiff, California Condor Recovery Team (CRT) Leader, announcing your intention to resign as of January 15, 1992, from the CRT. Your contributions to the recovery of the California condor over the last decade have been many and invaluable. Under your leadership, the Condor Captive Breeding Program at the San Diego Wild Animal Park pioneered the captive breeding techniques that enabled us to more than double the condor population in less than 5 years. The success of your efforts culminated in January of 1992, when the Fish and Wildlife Service (Service) released two captively bred condors. For the first time since AC-9 was captured in 1987, California condors flew free over the skies of southern California. You are one of a select few that can honestly say that you helped save the California condor from extinction. For that, you should feel very proud. The success of the Condor Program is due to the dedicated efforts of biologists like yourself, so it is with great regret that we accept your resignation.

The Service will continue to keep you informed of the progress of the recovery effort and hope we can call upon your expertise if required in the future.

Sincerely,

MARVIN L. P
Regional Director

For all of the political difficulties of the program, I am honored to have been a small part of it and cherish this letter.

Chapter 14

Falling in
LOVE
Diversifies My
WORLD
of
CONSERVATION

"There is a madness in loving you, a lack of reason
that makes it feel so flawless."
~*LEO CHRISTOPHER*

The few years leading up to the release of the California condors and my retirement from the recovery program had been tumultuous, to say the least. In 1993, when condors were first released back into the wild, I was thirty-seven years old. I had been part of a remarkable team that helped pull a spectacular bird back from the brink of extinction. I had achieved my childhood dream and become the curator of birds for the Zoological Society of San Diego. I had two amazing children and had been through a divorce.

My attention was now pulled in many directions, but none of them demanded more of my time and focus than falling in love. I had an early grade school experience of being in love and was completely heartbroken about a girl who did not love me. At best, she might have looked at me once, but nothing after that, so it probably wasn't a big deal, but it broke my heart. My younger sister, Barbara, and I shared clean-up responsibilities in the kitchen on the night when I decided to share my heartbreak. The story came out in choked sobs. My normally warm, coddling, protective Italian mom turned almost icy and chided, "You don't even know what it is like to be in love." Hurt and almost mad, I asked, "If this pain isn't it, how will I know when I am in love?" With an irritating non-answer, my mom simply assured, "You will know." I had always seen my mother as a woman of great wisdom, but this answer disappointed me. Sadly, it would be years before I understood her brilliance. I had a great love in my later teens but didn't have the support of my family. When my dad finally approved of someone I was dating, I married her. For Cyndi and me, our marriage had wonderful moments, including the birth of our two children, but in reality, not only had I married for my dad, but in too many ways, I felt I had married my dad. As the years went by, it simply didn't work. The divorce was difficult for many reasons, but the biggest was because it was the first really big personal decision I made on my own. Instead of following my parent's expectations or doing what my friends expected, I proceeded, knowing it would impact my work at the zoo and there would be widespread disapproval across the spectrum of relatives, friends, and colleagues. It was my first difficult adult decision, made by me and for me. Let's face it, men mature later than women, and even then, it continues to be a work in progress, but that's a whole other story.

Over the years at the Wild Animal Park, I had met a woman. To be more honest, I had only really seen this woman. She was not like any other. In some crazy way, she matched an image I had carried throughout childhood, puberty, and into my thirties. Tall, slender, with long brown hair, warm eyes, and a beautiful smile. That might seem shallow, and I cannot explain how it isn't, but it was like I had seen someone from a lifelong dream. It resonated in a very deep way I simply cannot explain. My mom's words rang in my ears—*you will know*—and somehow, I did. She was not without physical faults. She did seem to have unusually fat ankles, but I was generously willing to let that slide. It was only a short time later I learned she was wearing five-pound weights on each ankle in preparation for climbing Mt. Kilimanjaro. Now she was perfectly beautiful and liked to climb mountains. Then I knew for sure—she was my destiny.

Sunni Black was a Master Falconer, which was a real rarity among women, and worked for a company called Berwick Productions, which presented animal shows several times a day at the park. Her paperwork associated with the bird show went across my desk daily with reports on the condition of the birds in her care. Much like the little boy who pulls on a girl's ponytail or chases her with a snake to get her attention, I decided I should meet with her and correct the way she submitted her reports. Needless to say, we got off to a rocky start. Over time, we were able to have short conversations, but she really wasn't particularly interested in being romantically involved with me. I won't go through the litany of reasons for the rejection (it's too depressing) but rejected I was. Life shapes us all in different ways, and my life has taught me to be persistent and wait for opportunities.

She left on vacation with her mom and boyfriend, wine tasting in Australia and New Zealand, and I pined away the whole time. Her first day back at work, I spotted her and asked about her trip. Her eyes lit up. Her heart had been deeply touched by visiting a butterfly house in Melbourne. Never had she experienced such an amazing and emotionally touching phenomenon. It was at that precise moment I decided the Wild Animal Park needed a butterfly house, and I would be the one to make it happen.

I told everyone what a great exhibit it would be. In return, I was resoundingly told it would never happen by my mystified bird staff, my boss, the finance director, the operations director, the executive director, and ultimately, the board of directors. The Zoological Society was over seventy years old and had never displayed any invertebrates, and it wasn't going to start now. One day, on a walk through the Wild Animal Park with the president of the board of directors, I enthusiastically described my concept for a butterfly house and was left speechless by the response, "We only do animals here." It took every bit of restraint not to ask about our huge botanical collection or the clear taxonomic question of whether a butterfly was a plant or a rock. Only a year or so earlier, I had also gone nose-to-nose with the board over being able to use the word "evolution" in our graphics. Now this was the second time there was an erosion of my respect for the highly esteemed Zoological Society, but it just meant I had some work to do. I would need to be persistent. The zoo could grow and change. I was sure that the new butterfly house was a route to Sunni's heart, and I was not going to give up on either the house or her heart.

My persistence and passion would pay off on both fronts. Sunni was intrigued by my determination to press against seemingly insurmountable odds, and we began to date. Not too much or too fast. On our first date, I regaled her with all the things we could do together. She listened patiently for a bit, then put her hand on mine and said, "Let's get through this date before we plan another." I was in for a wild time and ultimately learned a lot from this woman.

One of our next dates took us to Pacific Grove, up the coast from where we lived, to tag monarch butterflies that were spending the winter resting in a eucalyptus grove. Tagging these migratory butterflies was an important part of being able to learn about their journey.

When we arrived, we were stunned to see clusters of hundreds of butterflies on one branch. A single tree could have thousands of resting butterflies. We carefully slipped long-handled nets around clusters of butterflies and lowered them to the ground. Then, sitting on blankets, we would evaluate each butterfly, record its estimated age, sex, and general condition, then place a tiny identifying tag on one wing. We could even determine if the female had recently mated.

Using our breath, we would warm the butterflies in our cupped hands and then release them back into the trees. The whole day rolled by as we tagged each butterfly, collecting data from them and warming them up enough that they could fly back up into the trees. We learned how to hold the butterflies and prepare them for the tagging process. The real pros were like Las Vegas card sharks dealing butterflies instead of aces and jacks. Butterflies with their wings neatly folded were lined up between each finger, ready to be flipped into place to be evaluated, tagged, and released. In quick motions, a "window" would be prepared by wiping the scales off one section of the wing and quickly applying a tag.

Okay, we skipped over that pretty deftly—determined if she has recently mated? Yes, that was what we did. During mating, the male deposited a mass or packet known as a spermatophore into the female. This packet carried the sperm, among other things, to fertilize the female's eggs. It could serve other important functions, depending on the species. In some butterflies, it contained nutrition for the female and therefore was often referred to as a "nuptial gift." It could also play a role in the competition to be the father. It was hypothesized that the first spermatophore placed in the female might serve as a dam, preventing other males' sperm from getting to the ovaries until it had dissolved and done its job. Healthy males often produced larger spermatophores, which might give their sperm the advantage. Apparently, in some cases, size mattered. Anyway, these spermatophores were significant enough that by gently palpating the female's abdomen, you could feel them and even count them. We should all be glad we are not butterflies.

It was a magical way to spend a day. While we were doing this, someone said, "If you think this is impressive, you should see what happens in Mexico!" And so began plans for an international date that would deeply affect my professional future.

At the same time, the Wild Animal Park was having a bad year and losing money left and right. I was in meeting after meeting about what the next new exhibit should be and how we could use it to bring in much-needed cash. The animal business was, in fact, just that, a business. Over the months, I had pushed hard enough on a butterfly house that the director finally pulled me aside. He had had enough. "Bill," he said, "the answer is no. The staff says no, the board says no, and I am saying no. If you bring up the b-word again, I will fire you." Even to me, that seemed like a relatively solid no.

Over the next few weeks, the meetings continued, and the management team was getting more desperate for an answer to the park's financial problems. A potential breakthrough came when someone made a contribution and designated it for building a hummingbird house at the park. As curator of birds, this donation fell into my court. In this gift, the leadership team saw hope for a new exhibit and a way to drive attendance. The gift was not enough money to complete it, but it was a solid start. It seemed like a hummingbird house would be a good idea to most of the staff. I was less impressed with the idea. The zoo's downtown campus had a hummingbird house, and it was popular, but not so popular it would drive attendance on its own. Hummingbirds were the butterfly of the bird world. In this opportunity, I saw a way to thread the needle.

During a short break, I found myself in the hallway outside of the boardroom where we had been meeting. The director was there.

A bit wary, I did not use the "b-word," but I suggested that with some modifications to traditional bird aviaries, we could build a hummingbird house that could hold non-avian flyers. With that, we could double down on our promotion. I was more than a little surprised when he quietly agreed, as long as it was kept quiet. After all, the board of trustees had said no butterflies.

While I was positively gleeful, I was also left in a difficult position. We needed a glass enclosure—a real greenhouse to maintain temperature and humidity—to keep tropical butterflies in San Diego. As we all know, birds and windows are most often a lethal combination, but for butterflies, windows are essential for temperature control. After some failed attempts at convincing the bird department that a glasshouse was a good idea for a hummingbird exhibit, I finally had to reveal the not-so-obvious brilliance of what I was doing. The keepers looked at me like I had gone crazy. My confession did little to salvage my reputation. It was clear that even with the door of opportunity cracked open, this would continue to be an uphill slog.

Finally, a glasshouse dubbed the Hidden Jungle rose from the ground and began to take shape. As the bird keepers learned what was going on, they got a little more cooperative but continued to shake their heads about birds in a glasshouse. We soaped the windows before we introduced birds so that they would have a chance to learn their limits. Tricky as it seemed, it turned out to be reasonably manageable for many birds. But, of course, this was not about birds. It was about love and butterflies. In the seventy-two hours before the exhibit opened, live butterflies chilled and sleeping in glassine envelopes arrived from all around the world and were placed in a refrigerator to hold the butterflies in torpor until opening day. As the butterflies were arriving and the exhibit was finally completed, I found Sunni and brought her in after hours and revealed the not-so-well-kept secret of a butterfly house. I had spread out a big blanket and loaded it with tasty treats and a bottle of chilled champagne. The butterflies opened their wings, and Sunni fell in love.

The day had finally come for the new Hidden Jungle to open. It had been advertised as a hummingbird house with never a mention of butterflies. Not one mention because it was taboo to mention any winged creature other than birds. But still, for my plans, there would need to be butterflies in the air when it opened, so I got up early and picked up Sunni to get to the park well before it opened. We had a lot of butterflies to warm up, wake up, and release. It was still two hours before the park opened, and we were still at least a mile away when the traffic stopped. It was early on a Saturday. There should've been no traffic problems. I felt in my heart that something horrible had happened on the curvy two-lane road to the park and hoped it didn't involve anyone I knew. People were literally out of their cars and walking around as they waited. With my heart in my stomach, I stopped a man walking past our car. "Do you know what has happened?" His reply was stunning. "Haven't you heard? There will be butterflies at the Wild Animal Park today!" Never had anything like this happened. My heart leapt from my stomach to my throat. This was unbelievable. I was giddy with excitement until I realized there would be no butterflies unless I could get around all this traffic to turn them loose.

We turned around and approached the park from the other side, bypassed the traffic, and drove in the employee entry. Sunni and I arrived breathlessly at the butterfly house and began releasing these beautiful flying flowers into the air. We were stuck underneath a deck in a hidden workroom that held the refrigerator and all the butterflies. Sitting in the cold, we would breathe on butterfly after butterfly and launch them into the air. Soon, the ground all around us was covered in sunning butterflies, but we didn't know what was actually happening in the exhibit. After a couple of hours, we were happy but cramped and cold. The park gates would open soon, and it was time for us to step out and see how it was working. We stood up and stepped out into the sunlit exhibit. The sight exceeded our dreams. The air was silently filled with colorful joy. Butterflies landed on flowers, branches, and our butterfly feeders. Our eyes simply could not sort it all out. The park guests apparently felt the same way. Lines wove through the whole forty-acre village for days. We had to regulate the number of people in the exhibit to prevent overcrowding. No one left disappointed, but no one went home happier than I did.

To this day, I have files of thank you notes from the director, the CFO, and even a few from board members. Amusingly, it was more than a decade before the Zoological Society officially approved the display of insects.

It might have taken a few years, but I learned what an unseemly business the animal business really was. Many curators today could do their business from behind a computer and be ignorant of what was really happening, or simply look the other way when it came to many of the awful things that occurred in animal transactions and captive management. Within zoos, this work was often carried out in the name of conservation, but a critical examination of the facts showed that this was rarely the outcome. Most animals living out their lives in zoos never contributed to the conservation of their species, except perhaps as animal ambassadors. Even with the California condor, we had yet to address the very issues that nearly drove it to extinction. Without doing that, we simply had the condor on expensive life support. Everyone, it seemed, was talking about conservation or studying declines of species or destruction of habitats, but no one was actually saving anything. I began to complain to all who would listen and even published articles criticizing zoos as an ineffective vehicle for real conservation. In the small world of zoos, I was not making many friends.

I am not sure why, but the last straw came in New Zealand. I was at an ornithological conference with some amazing biologists and ornithologists, such as Roger Tory Peterson and his wife. These were people I had looked up to all my life, but while they told stories of doom and gloom, there didn't seem to be anyone solving problems. Everyone was a researcher and piled study upon study to make the point about declining species, but had no solutions, no prescribed actions that actually addressed the root causes of animal extinctions. I am not sure what snapped, but somewhere during those meetings, I knew I was done. Zoos seemed so out of place in the conversation about conservation. Condors were a fluke when it came to captive roles in species recovery. In light of the thousands of disappearing species, our work on a handful seemed so wasteful. I was fully discouraged and without a clear direction. I knew what I wanted to do, but I could not do it in my "fantasy" job. After only ten years as curator of birds—a job I dreamed of since I was eight years old—I was done. Sunni and I returned to our hotel, and I announced I was quitting.

Once back in San Diego, I made an appointment with the executive director and informed him of my decision. We had long ago made amends, and though we frankly discussed differences in opinions over the years, we had developed a workable relationship. He accepted my resignation, asked me to write my ideal job description to share with other zoos and conservation organizations, and said he would help me find a new place in the world of conservation. The zoo always considered having an employee leave to work elsewhere as the equivalent of sending out an ambassador for all they did. That, along with my relatively controversial writing about the role of zoos, made it no surprise that he would be so eager to help me leave my current job.

Over the next couple of days, I wrote the job description and searched for places where I might find the kind of work I was looking for. I wrote about the importance of doing something other than research. It was time for action. The zoo had an enormous and brilliant staff studying issues in conservation, but no one, and I mean no one, actively implementing what we learned in a meaningful way. I wanted a team of "applied conservationists," people who would take the data and put it to work. At the next opportunity, I gave the description to the director. He sat and read every word while I quietly waited. He took his glasses off, leaned back in his chair, and said, "Okay, Bill, this is now your job. Please get to it and stop complaining." Although I did not leave the zoo, I made a major change in my career and was able to walk away from the past.

Falling in love had pushed me out of my comfort zone. I learned about butterflies and plants that I had somehow been able to ignore before. These new professional loves opened new doors for me that would ultimately redefine me as both a person and a biologist. This next ten-year span from the condor release in 1993 to 2003 would crush almost everything I understood of applied conservation biology. The incidents that occurred changed me as a human being. Thirty-six years with the zoo would soon be reduced to a memory.

But in this particular moment, I did not know that. I only knew that I was in charge of a new department and had to make a fresh start that would begin with monarch butterflies in Mexico and overlap with two other programs, one I would inherit in Paraguay and one of my own in Madagascar.

Chapter 15

MONARCH BUTTERFLIES

"Nature's message was always there and for us to see.
It was written on the wings of butterflies."
~KJELL B. SANDVED

Courting Sunni had obviously meant getting deeply involved with butterflies. The comment made by a stranger while we were tagging butterflies kept coming back. "If you think this is impressive, you should see what happens in Mexico!"

Monarch butterflies are the only migratory insect. In addition to that, there are two major US populations with two distinctly different migratory patterns. For many years, biologists had been familiar with the migration of the western population of monarchs. Each year, they would migrate from the Rocky Mountains west to the Pacific coast for the winter. By early spring, they would redistribute across their range and back to the mountains. But the migration of the eastern population—all the monarch butterflies from the Rocky

Mountains east—was a mystery until 1976. A young Fred Urquhart would watch the monarch butterflies at his home in Canada all summer long only to see them disappear across the border into the USA at the end of the summer. He was curious about where they went and ultimately became an entomologist. He, along with his wife Nora, dedicated their lives to discovering where this mass of butterflies went every winter.

Fred knew he needed a way to follow individual butterflies if he were to learn anything of value about their movements, so he immediately started searching for a way to tag them. Fortunately, monarch butterflies were relatively large, with an average wingspan of three inches, so it seemed reasonable they could carry a tiny paper tag. The trick was to attach this little tag to a delicate wing, be sure it would stay, and that the butterfly would not be damaged or otherwise impacted by the tag. He finally settled on a small paper circle about the size of a paper punch hole that had the same glue that was used to attach price tags in the grocery store. By rubbing the butterfly's scales off of its wings in a tiny area close to the body, he could stick the tag on and release the butterfly to go on its way across North America. Of course, he realized that North America was a huge continent, and if he hoped to get any tags back, he would need to tag hundreds of thousands and ultimately more than one million butterflies to get the information he needed. This also meant they could not do it alone.

Fred and Nora got everyone to help. They trained citizen scientists trying to tag the hundreds of thousands of butterflies in the hopes of retrieving a small handful of tags that might give some insights into the movements of the population. After years of work, the trail again went cold at the US/Mexico border, and it seemed time for Nora to step in with a fresh idea and give their search a big push. She placed a notice in a newspaper in Mexico that attracted the attention of Kenneth Brugger, a self-taught textiles expert and amateur naturalist.

Brugger was consulting in Mexico and courting a much younger Catalina Aguado, who had been born in the state of Michoacán. Catalina shared stories she had heard as a child about communities where people believed the spirits of their loved ones came back as butterflies. Every year on the Day of the Dead, millions of butterflies would come. This narrowed their search, and shortly thereafter, on a mountain called Cerro Pelón, a remarkable discovery was made. Not millions of butterflies or even tens of millions, but hundreds of millions of butterflies covered oyamel fir trees—more butterflies than the human eye and mind could comprehend.

Fred and Nora traveled from Canada to Mexico to see if these were the butterflies they had spent decades searching for. The butterfly colonies were located at an altitude of ten thousand feet. The lack of oxygen exhausted Fred. With these enormous numbers of butterflies, the ground was littered with the normal fatalities one might expect. For a good scientist, it was not enough to find hundreds of millions of butterflies. To be certain that these were the butterflies he had been tracking, he had to find one of "his" butterflies. Because of the sheer number of butterflies, the odds of finding one of the relatively few tagged butterflies were stacked enormously against them. Fred was sixty-five years old and suffering from a heart condition. The story was that Fred sat on a stump to catch his breath and, while doing so, stirred a small pile of dead butterflies with his walking stick. There, at that moment, he, fortunately, found a butterfly wearing his familiar tag. PS 397 had

If the forest is the cathedral, the butterflies are its stained glass windows.

been tagged and released by two schoolboys and their teacher in Chaska, Minnesota, in 1975. With that discovery, the search he had devoted a lifetime to had finally come to an end.

Sunni and I made our first journey to Mexico only thirteen years after the overwintering sites had been discovered. We arrived in the small colonial town of Angangueo in the state of Michoacán. Angangueo was a small but spectacularly beautiful community: cobblestone roads, beautiful buildings of dusty rose-colored limestone, and well-kept homes with balconies adorned with geraniums. We checked in at the Hotel Don Bruno and excitedly waited for a ride to El Rosario, the largest of the public butterfly sanctuaries.

It would be an understatement to say that we were unprepared for what we saw. Pathways of flying butterflies in swirling orange and black clouds so dense they literally took your breath away. The same instinct that prevents you from breathing when you put your face in

For more than thirty years, Sunni and I have bathed in swarms of overwintering monarchs and have learned how incredible such a connection to nature can be.

water can kick in when thousands of butterflies swirl around your face. The trees themselves were completely covered in butterflies from the top to the bottom, branches and trunks nothing but shivering beautiful butterflies. Standing at the feet of evenly spaced ancient oyamel fir trees brought to life by millions of fluttering butterflies easily put any man-made cathedral to shame. Where Pacific Grove could proudly boast ten to twenty thousand butterflies, the forests of Mexico boasted one billion butterflies, over 550 tons, blanketing the boughs of the oyamel fir trees.

We cried, we laughed, and we worked. We tagged thousands of butterflies to help estimate the population size and track their journey north. We were moved—no, we were changed. Our lives would never be the same. Though the visual phenomenon was different, we were moved as I had been moved when I saw my first condor. Understanding and protecting this phenomenon was now a priority and a new adventure in our conservation story.

The magic of this phenomenon cannot be overstated. Imagine a butterfly emerging from its chrysalis somewhere in southern Canada during the late summer months. That butterfly would be in reproductive diapause, called the Methuselah stage. This simply means that it will not be reproductively active during this time. Instead, all its energy is poured into an extended life that will allow it to fly south for up to three thousand miles until it arrives at the oyamel fir forests high in the mountains of Central Mexico. Other monarchs from all across eastern North America join it along its route until they all arrive in Mexico, one billion strong. It is not just that all these butterflies get to the same place, but they all get there at the same time. Within weeks of each other, they all gather in the forest. To make this even more remarkable, these butterflies have never been to this forest before or even to Mexico, and neither have their parents, their grandparents, or their great-grandparents.

Here they spend the winter wrapped in the protective cloak of an ancient oyamel fir forest.

As spring approaches, the butterflies slowly warm up. Those that survived the thousands of miles of flying and the long, frigid winter are dehydrated and hungry. By late February, butterflies are pouring in and out of the roost trees, searching for water and nectar to replenish themselves. At the same time, they abandon sexual diapause. The males pursue the females and seal their fate as they begin to mate. There is no native milkweed in the mountains, and the butterflies will use up the last bits of their energy to fly north to the nearest milkweed, where they will lay their eggs and most will die. Their offspring continue the mating and journey north until two or three generations later, the monarch is redistributed across North America. Then it all starts again.

Chapter 16

PROTECTING
the
MONARCH'S
FOREST

"Everyone has a thousand wishes before a tragedy,
but just one afterward."

-FREDRIK BACKMAN

Now our challenge was to design a conservation program. This was a bit outside the zoo's core abilities—captive breeding, in and of itself, was not a conservation program, and breeding monarchs in captivity was not going to be the solution to this problem. The forest that was so vital to the survival of the overwintering butterflies had been eroded over the years.

This forest had shrouded the mountains and provided life-giving water to growing cities from its rich watershed, timber for construction, and fuel for cooking fires for as long as anyone could remember. It was a designated World Heritage site and protected under Mexican law by some of the best environmental laws in the world. Still, the challenges in Mexico were many. Despite the quality of the legislation, corruption had made the laws essentially unenforceable. Over the years, we had seen cycles of forest loss due to illegal logging activities. Like drug cartels, the logging cartels all too often worked with near impunity. I had personally seen law enforcement officers discipline an older woman for littering while trucks loaded with trees stolen from the forest drove down the main street. In fairness, the loggers were often armed, and the little old lady likely was not.

Our challenge was to design a program that would educate the local community about the value of the butterfly phenomenon and the worth of a healthy forest. The next few years would be interesting. The World Wildlife Fund launched a tree planting program, where they would pay farmers to take seedlings to plant on their property. It was not too hard to see where that was going to go. We drove around collecting trees that had been dumped by the truckload into ditches around the reserves and delivering them to any nursery that was interested. By the end of that program, trees were purchased, farmers were paid, and there was not much to show in the way of results.

To the local people, the only time a tree was valuable was when you could sell it. Technically, the protected status of the forest was stealing that value from some of Mexico's most underserved communities—the indigenous people living on *ejidos*, land granted to them by the government to support themselves. Whether it was illegal logging for a small income or cutting firewood to cook for their family, these were processes essential to their way of life. It was here that I was first exposed, albeit unknowingly, to the concept of environmental refugees.

To develop local relationships, my colleagues and I spent many nights sipping beer and sitting on orange crates playing checkers with old farmers or conducting community classes to train guides for the reserves. In the zoo's education department, I found a sympathetic partner, and together we helped fund and build interpretive centers. Working with women on the boundary of the reserves, we taught pine needle basketry and encouraged them to sell baskets to tourists. These were made from a little piece of the forest that was easily replenished and provided some much-needed income.

We knew we could not directly impact illegal logging activity, but we also knew they were not the only threat to these ancient forests. Every year, people harvested hundreds of thousands of trees for firewood. This harvest was at least as destructive as the loss of forest to loggers.

The collection of fuelwoods by local families and small businesses was most often portrayed as picking up dead branches off the forest floor. Tragically, this was rarely the case. It was legal to take dead trees from the forest, so many trees were killed by girdling the tree. The bark and life-giving cambium layers were removed around the base, causing it to die. Other trees were cut outright then into firewood where they fell. The wood carried by people, horses, and burros clearly showed the clean cut of a saw, but it was too late for enforcement. It was estimated that a single family would harvest an average of twenty trees per year for their cooking and heating fires.

There was clearly a complex and intimate relationship among these forests, the people, and the monarch butterfly. These forests served not only the people but were also critical to the overwintering butterflies. All summer long, the massive fir trees soaked up the summer sun. As the butterflies arrived in the fall and searched out the oyamel fir trees, one could easily imagine a warmth-sharing phenomenon as the butterflies blanketed the trees in the same way the trees blanketed the mountain and buffered the cold winter temperatures. The harvest of trees, whether for timber or fuel, threatened

*With more than three billion people around the world harvesting wood
for fires, the impact on habitats and climate change is stunning.*

the function in the same manner that holes in a blanket lessened its
effectiveness. That relationship between the forest, people, and the
butterfly collapsed one night with catastrophic consequences.

On January 13, 2002, when I arrived to visit the butterflies at El
Rosario, my Mexican colleagues were somber. Beyond that, they gave
no indication of what I was about to see. We wandered into the forest.
I was struck by how many dead butterflies I saw, but there were always
dead butterflies in the reserves. This turned out to be different. As we
went deeper into the reserve, things changed quickly. We saw tens
of thousands of dead butterflies, then hundreds of thousands, then
millions, tens of millions, and finally, hundreds of millions of dead
monarchs. Sounds of the forest were muffled but for the noise of the
crunching of wings underfoot. The floor of the reserve was thickly
carpeted with carcasses of millions upon millions of monarchs, victims
of a freeze turned deadly thanks to the destruction of the protective
forest. It was no wonder my colleagues were silent. Nothing could have
prepared us for what we saw: dead butterflies laying up to thirty inches
deep at the roots of the fir trees, like orange and black snow.

On January 11, 2002, a cold, wet storm had swept through the mountains. Freezing rain followed by strong winds blowing through the holes in the forest blanket took their toll on the sleeping monarchs. An estimated 270 million monarch butterflies—about 25% of the migratory population of the eastern monarch butterfly—had died in one night.

That winter, El Rosario earned a new nickname from locals. Someone even decided to redesign the preserve's entry sign with it. They took a piece of charcoal, drew a rough black cross through "El Rosario," and wrote the new name beneath it: "El Cementerio." It was likely that the artist was unaware of the irony underlying his actions. The charcoal he'd chosen as his medium was the byproduct of the very thing that had killed the butterflies in the first place.

My colleague, Tom Hanscom, and I spoke out and published an article about the failure of conservation groups to address the

In one day, the remarkable forest cathedral was turned into a killing ground. Piles of dead butterflies were strewn about like broken shards of stained glass.

core issues that led to the destruction of the forest. The response from the conservation community was not so much defensive as vitriolic. Dr. Lincoln Brower—my generation's monarch butterfly guru and academic—struck back harshly, as did the World Wildlife Fund in Mexico.

The World Wildlife Fund had little to show for decades of work and millions of donor dollars invested. They were understandably defensive, but as the elephant in the room, they never backed down. Dr. Brower was first and foremost a scientist. He always reported data and never spoke out about the issues, despite having a powerful place in the spotlight. It reminded me in so many ways of how scientists in the condor program had tried to communicate. Ultimately Dr. Brower and I were able to sit down and finally talk it through. To Dr. Brower's credit, he adjusted his way of thinking when I explained my logic and accepted a couple of my suggestions. Thereafter, he made some notable changes in how he communicated what he knew about butterflies. After our conversation, Dr. Bower's interviews became more dynamic. He was more direct about the problems facing the butterflies and became an even more powerful spokesperson for change. But for the butterflies, that was about all that changed.

There had been a time when the zoo and park really engaged and supported the programs in Mexico. Sunni and I worked closely with the education department at the zoo, developed material for the Mexican guides, and helped fund and build interpretive centers at the butterfly reserves. The zoo's merchandising department started carrying baskets from pine needles made by local artisans, hoping to instill a sense of continuing value in a tree that could be an ongoing resource. Marketing and public relations got involved, and the zoo even led tours to see the butterflies. With all this going on, there was a feeling of success you get around people all dancing to the same drum, but this catastrophe changed everything. Our outreach had not changed behaviors. Our work had not stopped the cutting. We had not saved the butterflies. Collectively, we had all failed. Our tactics failed to change in light of the horrific demonstration of catastrophic death. In a sad way, the condor program seemed easy and hopeful in retrospect. The conservation of butterflies and the bigger problems facing the world were profoundly overwhelming.

Chapter 17

PARAGUAY, THE LAST STRAW

"Paraguay is nowhere and famous for nothing."
~PJ O'ROURKE

The California condor program and those projects that followed honed my political skills. The Zoological Society made use of those skills in delicate situations, and I was always proud of being able to help. When I was asked to step into a politically troubled program in Paraguay, I found myself more challenged and confused than ever before—not by the biology, but by the entire program, its collaborators, and its reasons for existing.

The intention of this chapter, edited out for legal reasons, was to share the last of the three stories of failure that would ultimately cause me to leave my dream job. Suffice it to say, I was left completely disillusioned and lost. I had an empty, nowhere-to-turn feeling. It was like I was an orphan within my professional family, but the family was still there, watching me. No one stepped forward to help. I was left very alone.

I was done. It was really time to walk away. I just needed time to figure out where to go.

The experiences in Paraguay were so sadly wicked. This orphaned anteater, its mother killed by hunters, brought a moment of light and caring.

Chapter 18

Madagascar–
OUTSIDE
THE CIRCLE
OF FIRE

"Without the forest, there will be no more water,
without water, there will be no more rice."
-MADAGASCAR PROVERB

Through my growing focus on tropical fieldwork, including in Borneo and Papua New Guinea, I had unknowingly been establishing a reputation for myself as someone comfortable and competent in remote fieldwork. Sunni had broadened my biological interests to the point that I was an amateur expert in insects, particularly tropical butterflies. My work with zoo researchers and post-doctoral students got me involved with everything from Bahamian iguanas to giant armadillos in Argentina. Each new project and location honed my skills. Every new destination was exciting, but a phone call from Claire Kremen in early 1995 electrified me. Claire was representing a consortium made up of USAID, CARE International, the Wildlife Conservation Society, and the government of Madagascar. We spoke briefly about my experience with fieldwork in general and butterflies in particular. Then, the reason for her call. "Would you be willing to lead an expedition across the Masoala Peninsula in northeastern Madagascar?" I felt a wave of excitement ripple through me. I thought briefly of Art Risser asking me if I knew how to raise a baby condor, and once again, I immediately answered, "Yes!"

I probably was not the most qualified person for the job, but then, maybe I was. This was like the condor program, potentially huge and something I knew I could be passionate about. Madagascar is a paradise for biologists and is situated just off the east coast of Africa near Mozambique. While it is a big island, the fourth largest island in the world, it still has a relatively small landmass of only 226,000 square miles. Yet, it is packed with unique species of plants and animals. I can only describe Madagascar as being magically Seussical, the only place that might have provided a challenge for the creative genius of Dr. Seuss' characters. There are 202 species of chameleons distributed through much of the Old World; more than half of them are found in Madagascar and 59 of those are ONLY in Madagascar. There are roughly 100 species of lemurs, and this entire family of primates is only found in Madagascar. Its north-south orientation allows for diverse habitats, ranging from dry deserts and stone forests in the south to luxuriant rainforests in the far north. This amazing diversity is so great that it makes its continental neighbor of Africa look biologically impoverished in every way but one. The destruction of Madagascar's habitats and its wildlife is nearly complete, and with this loss of resources comes human poverty. A visit to Madagascar brings you face-to-face with a horrific spectacle of both beautiful and tragic things often intimately entwined.

The Masoala Peninsula was the largest remaining patch of tropical rainforest left in Madagascar. Most of it was still pristine, a quality that was hard to find in a rainforest anywhere in the world. It was a little over one hundred miles across with a modest mountain chain with an altitude of a little over four thousand feet down the middle and a rugged coastline, mountains, and rainforest. We had every reason to believe that the journey would be filled with diverse wildlife, beautiful scenery, and interesting adventures.

Qualified or not, YES, I was willing to lead an expedition. Without hesitation, I launched directly into preparing for the trip, the first step in a multi-year journey that included everything we hoped for and changed me and the rest of my life in ways I could not possibly have prepared for.

Preparations for an extended expedition could be challenging. You needed to be conscious of weight but certain of having everything you might need. Lists were made and remade. We shopped, changed our minds, returned things, and shopped again. Water was essential but far too heavy to carry, so we purchased expensive, lightweight, medical-grade water filters. We also bought tents, leech-proof socks, mosquito nets, mosquito repellants, sleeping sheets, and so much more. Only when the door of the jet leaving San Diego was shut and you taxied to the runway, did you finally lean back and heave a sigh of relief. If you forgot something, it's too late. In the end, you pat your pockets, check for your passport and credit cards, and away you go.

By fall, Sunni and I were on our way to Madagascar. The island is almost perfectly antipodal to San Diego—using a globe, if you put one finger on our home in San Diego and another on the Masoala Peninsula, you could easily spin the globe. It would be hard to be any further from home without standing in the Indian Ocean just off the coast of Madagascar. Two days after we had left home, the pilot announced we would soon be beginning our descent into Antananarivo, Madagascar. We stared anxiously out the cracked and yellowed coach class windows into the inky darkness, hoping to see some indication we were finally nearing our destination. I expected city lights, but instead, I saw giant circles of fire all over the landscape. Circle after circle surrounded only by darkness. What was outside of these circles of fire?

With my heart literally fluttering with excitement, nervousness, and even a touch of fear, we touched down on the runway and taxied to a stop. As the doors opened, the cold cabin air was quickly replaced by warm, smoky air. We exited into the night and onto the poorly lit tarmac. It was like so many other hot, humid airport terminals in developing countries. It struck me that no matter how often you did this, being somewhere where everything was so different made you anxious. To the uninitiated, arrival at the terminal was nothing less than terrifying. Like sheep, we followed the person in front of us and hoped for the best. The airport terminal was dingy, hot, and dark. The immigration officer looked suspicious and angry. I immediately felt like a criminal trying to sneak something past them, and from the way it looked, they were equally suspicious. They glared at my passport with an attitude that suggested they were trying to keep us out as opposed to letting us in. They thumbed through the pages so slowly I was sure they were looking for something bad and predetermined they would find it. My passport had only two blank pages. In the opinion of the immigration officer, that was not space enough to accommodate multiple huge arrival stamps.

I was initially frightened when he told me I could not enter the country and would have to return to Paris. I calmed down quickly when it occurred to me that the plane I had arrived on was already loading to leave and would not be back for two days. It was the only flight in and out of the country. When I did not turn away, I was simply ignored. Finally, when the last passengers had gone through and I was the only person left standing in the immigration lounge, he called me over and finally stamped my passport. I learned later while describing the incident to someone more experienced in the ways of Madagascar that "greasing his palm" would have sped things up, but I was naive to the ways of Madagascar. The officer finally gave up waiting for me to figure it out.

The baggage claim area was packed with far more people than had been on our flight. Locals were all looking for a way to make a dollar, and "helping" the tourists was an irresistible opportunity. It was not a managed or licensed process, so tons of people just showed up when flights came in. Luggage was grabbed and hauled off. Fortunately, we found ours and went through customs, then stepped into pitch black nighttime chaos. People in dirty, torn clothes grabbed at our bags and offered us rides in a variety of languages as they tried to figure out where we were from and what language we spoke. It felt every bit as disorganized and edgy as it looked. Fortunately, we were quickly rounded up by several staff members from Project Masoala and hustled into a car. Our luggage had disappeared, but we were assured that people on our "team" had the bags.

In the midst of all this turmoil, I heard a familiar and lovable greeting, "Hey, Billy boy! How are ya?" followed by a heartfelt and somewhat odoriferous hug. It was Roy Toft, a colorful and immensely talented wildlife photographer with a black belt in karate, absolutely no sense of personal distance, an insatiable appetite, and a noisy, gregarious personality. Way less concerned about his personal grooming than getting the job done and having a good time, he could be a mixed bag, to say the least, but these are the people I love. Roy could be short-tempered and impatient with people, but he could sit quietly in a blind forever with infinite and forgiving patience for all things wild. Roy had wrapped up a long and exhausting photo expedition in East Africa a week or so earlier and had flown ahead to Madagascar to meet us. With no particular plan in mind while he waited for us, he moved in with a small family desperate enough to take him as a guest and spent his days playing ball with grimy but perpetually happy street kids until we arrived.

Roy had worked with Sunni years earlier at the bird show and had presented birds on stage for many years. He loved birds but loved wildlife photography even more. During my condor years, Nick Nichols, a celebrated wildlife photographer, came to town to assist National Geographic with a story. I connected Roy with Nick, and they hit it off. The next thing I knew, Roy was on his way to India to assist Nick with a story on tigers. Roy had his first opportunity as a professional photographer, and over the years, he just kept getting better at his art. Because of that and our comfortable friendship, he would be my companion throughout the trek across the peninsula.

Once in the car and out of the airport, we were onto dark, dirty, poorly maintained streets. In the middle of the night, it was mostly quiet, but everything we saw or smelled spoke of poverty. Small children bundled in rags slept alone along the roadside. Families huddled together for warmth around a small fire with no shelter in sight. Sad, brutal, and at the same time, beautiful. It was fascinating to watch the nighttime landscape go by. Small, tall homes set out into rice paddies, piles of homemade bricks all along the red, dusty roads, a combination of pride and desperation. Madagascar was once a French colony, and as we approached the city of Antananarivo, you could see the fading beauty of the city's architecture. The Malagasy were not fond of the French. Once they gained their independence, they showed little respect for things left by the French—buildings, schools, and roads. During our time in Madagascar, there were actually fewer roads than there were in the 1960s. Much of what the French left behind, including much of the school system, was abandoned or allowed to fall into disrepair.

Finally, we approached the core area of the city. A middle-aged woman hiked up her dress and defecated in the street as we pulled up in front of the famous Hôtel Colbert near the heart of downtown. Hôtel Colbert wasn't really famous except to biologists. Everyone who was with an NGO doing research or conservation in Madagascar would, at some point, stay at the Hôtel Colbert. Gerald Durrell,

OBE, the famous British naturalist, author, and conservationist, had often stayed there and, because of that alone, it was simply the place to be.

It had a patio bar and, like most of the hotels Sunni and I stayed in, had more mosquitoes in the room and patios than we ever encountered in the forest. Over the years, whether it was Papua New Guinea, Cameroon, or Honduras, Sunni and I often would check into our room and make the bed by pitching our tents right on top of the mattress. This saved us from innumerable uncomfortable issues, ranging from damp to wet mattresses, moldy linens, bed bugs, mosquitoes, botflies, and other pests.

In the evening, the doormen of the Hôtel Colbert watched us cautiously when we left, warning us not to walk too far. One went so far as to tell us we would be killed and then robbed, not the other way around. While somewhat of an exaggeration, it was clear that in such an impoverished place, even simple objects I had might well be worth my life to someone else.

There was a great outdoor pizza place diagonally across the street. It wasn't a structure but an area of sidewalk sheltered by multiple old tarps strung as a roof. It was classically outfitted with rickety folding chairs and plastic tables with sticky plastic tablecloths. Most of their clientele were prostitutes or travelers like us, looking for a cheap, familiar meal. The pizza was pretty tasty; they had cold Three Horses Beer in large bottles; and the people watching was good. It became a regular spot for food whenever we were in the city. The doormen never grew comfortable with us going there. Whenever we went, they would watch our every move and run to escort us back when they saw us finish our meals.

Just down the hill from the hotel was the famous outdoor market known as the Zoma. The Zoma was the world's largest outdoor market, and in a dangerous city, it was also the epicenter of crime. Anything you could want or need was in the Zoma. Animals were butchered, rice was threshed, and spices were sold. In areas of the

Zoma, the delicious odors and beautiful colors exuding from spice, fabric, and flower stands clashed with the bawling of terrified animals and the terrible sights and odors associated with an abattoir. Roy and I went to shoot some photos, but we were overwhelmed by waves of nausea and decided our memories would serve us as well as any photos!

We had a few days in "Tana," as the capital was called by locals, and as nice as the hotel was, we wanted to get out and explore. Once administrative details were settled in the city, we were off to our first experience in the bush. Time was money. The program was funded well enough that, instead of endless days on terrible roads in rickety cars, we were able to book flights on Air Madagascar. We quickly learned that the internal flights on Air Madagascar were always exciting. It started with a guessing game as to whether or not the flight would show up and usually ended with wondering if it would land in the general region of where it was supposed to go. We headed off to the airport, hoping to catch a flight to Maroantsetra. True to Air Madagascar's reputation, we found ourselves with a day or two in Tamatave, a port city in the same general direction as Maroantsetra, but not quite there. Since Maroantsetra was accessible only by boat or air, we had no choice but to wait until Air Mad decided we would go the rest of the way.

A day or two later, there was a rumor of a flight to complete our trip, and we headed off to the airport. Even away from the capital city, the overwhelming poverty of Madagascar permeated everything, and waiting at the airport provided no relief. True to form, Air Madagascar had not yet decided if it was going to show up, or if it did, there was no assurance that it would take off. Our tiny group of six people sat at a table having a drink while we waited for news about our flight. From across the room, I could see a dark-haired woman in shabby clothes targeting our table. I knew she was going to ask us for food, money, or both. Being somewhat paternal and watching out for my little team, I warned them by saying, "Just ignore her, and she will go away." That actually worked quite well in many instances, but not this one. She walked directly up to our table and, in perfect English, said, "Aren't you Bill Toone?" Well, there stood a very disheveled Dr. Eleanor Sterling. She had volunteered for me with the California condor program years earlier in San Diego. Since then, she had attended Duke University and had spent two years living in a tent on the tiny island of Nosy Mangabe, an island that at low tide was literally walking distance from Maroantsetra. It was on this tiny island that she was doing post-doctoral research on Madagascar's most unusual lemur, the aye-aye.

The aye-aye is a remarkable and generally controversial animal. Taxonomists have battled over whether it is a rodent, a primate, or something unique among all the options. Many locals believe that seeing one is a bad omen and kill them on sight. At one time, they were thought to be extinct, but now it seems that there are certainly more of this unusual nocturnal lemur than anyone had expected. So they are strange and rare enough we thought it would be great to see one. Eleanor sat down, drew a remarkably detailed map of the island, gave us exact times and explicit directions, and off she went to catch her next flight.

At long last, we flew from Tamatave to Maroantsetra. Maroantsetra was in the armpit formed by the Masoala Peninsula and the mainland; it sat right on the shores of the Bay of Antongil. Although the market town of Maroantsetra was the primary access point to the peninsula, it was really only accessible by air or boat. It was here that Project Masoala had a small home. We settled in for a few days of acclimation and orientation before Roy and I headed off on our trek. Once we were on our way, Sunni planned to catch a flight back to the capital city and then home, where her anxious mother would meet her.

First on our list was a camping expedition to Nosy Mangabe to visit Eleanor's campsite and try to see the mysterious and elusive aye-aye. This would be a short but nerve-jangling ride in a pirogue, a dugout canoe. Sunni and I had previous experiences in dugout canoes from Papua New Guinea, so we had a general sense of what we were in for. The Papuan dugouts were usually equipped with outriggers, making them both harder to tip over and harder to steer. At least that was our assessment. The Malagasy dugouts did not have an outrigger, and as best as I could tell, the boatmen kept them upright with counterintuitive moves. They were generally poled by someone standing in the back. My experience in proper canoes was to use your body as a counterbalance if you felt the canoe tipping. Apparently, this was not the system in a pirogue; counterbalancing messed with the guy trying to pole the boat, and so you had to lean with the dugout as opposed to against it. Filling them up with gear only made things dicier. The program director, Claire Kremen, Sunni, Roy, and I piled into two dugouts and set off for the island. It was a blessedly uneventful trip that ended with the soft sound of the canoe sliding into a beautiful sand beach, where there was a small clearing surrounded by forest.

The sun was preparing to set, and the waters of the bay were lapping against the shore of the tiny island. In the forest behind us, black-and-white lemurs were barking out territorial messages, toads and frogs were doing harmony, and the first of the fireflies were morse-coding with light to all who could interpret the message.

An important rule of rainforest camping is to camp in a clearing. Sometimes the broiling tropical sun makes this seem like an odd choice, but having a large branch or tree fall on your tent is generally worse than having to put on sunblock. Once we were all set up, we pulled out Eleanor's map and instructions. She had literally tagged every significant tree on the island. She had rustic benches in key areas, and her directions were explicit. As detailed as, "Go to this bench at this time. At 9:15, the aye-aye will come from tree thirty-three on this branch and pass above the bench." Shortly after sunset, on our first night out in the forest, we were off in search of an aye-aye—a search many scientists had failed, but we had the inside scoop thanks to our chance meeting with Eleanor.

We trudged up the mountain, following one of Eleanor's trails. For some reason, all her trails went up the mountain. Never were they flat or, for that matter, downhill, or at least that was how it seemed. We spotted some significant bones at the base of a tree. There were not many large animals in Madagascar, so I commented, and we stopped. Our guide quietly said, "Oh, those bones. This is a cemetery." I reacted in disbelief. If this was a cemetery, then someone was digging up the dead people! Our guide gently explained the local rituals. Bodies were never buried. Shortly after death, the deceased would be wrapped up and placed under a tree. Family and friends would mourn the dead and party with them in a ceremony often referred to as the turning of the bones. It would not be unusual to have continued contact with the body. Often, empty bottles of alcohol lying around would attest to the activities of the night before. I was still unconvinced until a smiling guide pointed to a small, rotted box. The lid had caved in over the years. When I peered in, I found myself eye to eye socket with a human skull. After about one year, the

There is an amazing intimacy with death throughout Madagascar.
After my centipede bite, I was told I could die and remain in
the village of Antanambao.

body was rewrapped and put into a small box—by then, everything could be folded up and stacked. For the poorest of the Malagasy, the small box is made of wood, and now more and more often, you see small cement caskets, but they are never buried. How would you visit and party if they were buried? Food for thought while we continued our walk.

Just in time, we found her bench, sat down, got ourselves oriented, and waited for the aye-aye to appear. They are truly bizarre animals, and one can see how they might be the devil or worse. An adult aye-aye weighs about five pounds and is about three feet long, making them the world's largest nocturnal primate. They have rodent-like front incisors that never stop growing, a long furry tail, and a bizarrely thin middle finger they use to tap on trees.

Creeping along the branches, the aye-aye taps the tree at a rate of about eight taps per second. Using echolocation, it listens for hollow spots and the movement of grubs, which would make a tasty bite. Once it locates a hollow, it uses its incisors to make a hole in the tree. It is then that this skinny little finger really gets put to work. It slips that bony finger into the hollow and feels around for grubs, which it pulls out and eats.

As we sat quietly in the darkness, skeptically waiting for this ghost of the night, I grew cynical about our chances of success. So many people looked for the aye-aye, and most never found one. The time clicked by, and 9:15 was seconds away when sure enough, rapid taps, a pause, and more rapid taps. At that precise moment, the shadowy aye-aye appeared above our heads. We just held our breath and watched. He moved along slowly and methodically. The shadows finally stole him from our view, and the sounds of insects filled the night air as the rhythmic tapping faded away.

After a couple of days, we headed back to Maroantsetra and Project Masoala's rented home. Food in the form of protein was not abundant, but rice was a staple. Three times a day, a local Malagasy woman would show up at the house and prepare meals for our team. Lots of rice and occasionally a bit of meat—mostly chicken. She never called us to a meal. The food would be put out, and she would disappear. This gave Roy, with his ability to sense unprotected food, an unfortunate advantage over the rest of us. We rolled into the house one day, and Roy, perpetually missing his shirt, managed to wolf down nearly every piece of chicken before anyone else knew it was there.

The tiny house was cramped. Sunni and I got a room to ourselves as a married couple, and everyone else made do with whatever other space was available. Located just on the edge of the community, we could hear a lot of the goings-on around us. The constant stream of chatty people passing by didn't fully prepare us for one particular pre-dawn event. We were panicked by the screams of a woman so deep, guttural, and painful that we were simultaneously jerked up from bed and nearly nauseous by the agonizing sound. There was a horrific sense of helplessness. We did not speak the language. We were strangers in the community, and other than Roy, probably poorly prepared to step into what must have been a vicious confrontation. But then, as quickly as the screams started, there was dead silence. It was a silence with an empty finality to it. There was no doubt the screams would not start up again. It was not until breakfast we learned with some relief that the screams came from a pig being slaughtered—bad enough, but at least not a helpless woman.

Then it was time for our trek to begin. Roy and I left the town of Maroantsetra in the pouring rain. Our pirogue made the wet trip to a trail that led into the mountains. In no time at all, we, our bags, and a hired guide from the park service were unceremoniously dumped on the sandy beach. We barely had the last of our bags off the boat before they pushed off and headed back for the mainland.

For a variety of reasons, most of the trekking team, other than Roy, would either cancel before the trek started or early on as they realized the challenges we would face. The most critical person we lost, aside from our guide, was our translator, and losing that pivotal position led to a mass resignation of our porters. The fact that none of us knew where we were going and no one spoke Malagasy was more than they were willing to deal with. We picked up our stuff and simply walked to the next village. In a place with no employment, we knew we could find some help, and we did.

Our trek started by walking into what felt like an idyllic piece of art. Green mist laced hills, sprawling rice paddies, and little villages with lazy curls of cooking smoke leaking through the walls before blending into the tropical mist. Even the tiny villages were a veritable beehive of activity, with people working in the rice paddies, women hovering over cooking fires, men repairing their fragile homes, while the kids played and herded chickens and zebu cows. The Malagasy dialect of the Masoala had a wonderful sing-song lilt to it. In the wee hours, as the ladies walked to the rice paddies for a long day of work, their conversations sounded more like happy songs. It was beautifully serene along the shores of the bay. As we trekked towards the mountains, the rice paddies became less frequent, and the forest began to more consistently embrace our trail.

Our small band of porters leaving the coast behind us and heading to the forest of the Masoala Peninsula.

Sadly, rivers were seen as a toilet that you could bathe in, along with washing dishes and clothes. For us, this was an ongoing health risk wherever there were people. We quickly learned that many parts of their lives were controlled by things that were "fady," bad luck. High on that list was drinking anything cold—presumably a direct response to waterborne illnesses. Our water filters were excellent and safe to use, but after seeing the quantities of human waste going into the river, boiling the water was an extra precaution that seemed worthwhile.

Throughout Madagascar, rice was a staple. On the Masoala Peninsula, it was pretty much all that anyone ate. After cooking the rice, the ladies would allow the layer of rice left in the bottom of the pot to lightly toast. To that, they would add water and boil. It created a rice tea called ranonapango and, thanks to the fady about cold drinks, was pretty much all the local people ever drank.

I had prepared for every eventuality on this trek. A good rule for packing is the rule of three. Especially with clothing, three is the most you will really need of any one thing. Three light long-sleeved shirts for sun protection, three long pants for protection from thorns and nettles, three pairs of leech-proof socks to avoid the little bloodsuckers.

Invariably, you find there was one thing you did not plan on, and in this case, I had not planned on wading across streams several times a day. Wearing all my jungle paraphernalia became a huge problem. We would hike for an hour or so and then encounter a stream. That meant we sat down and removed our comfortable boots, leech-proof socks, and long pants to avoid walking all day in wet gear. On the other side of the stream, everything had to go back on. The porters could only look on in wonder as we repeated this ritual each time we encountered water.

After a day or two of this, it occurred to me it was probably a good thing I did not understand Malagasy. The looks of wonder the porters wore at first slowly dissolved. Their patience waiting for Roy and me at every stream quickly waned. Finally, we found ourselves playing catch up with the porters. Seeing as we didn't know where we were going, and they were carrying all of our stuff, it seemed like jungle hide-n-seek might not be such a good idea. After one final crossing, the long pants, the leech-proof socks, and my nice boots were all left in a pile. We completed the trek in shorts, t-shirts, and flip-flops.

We were finally seeing nearly pristine habitats. The forest turned rich and vibrant, and the signs of people were reduced to the narrow path we were following deeper into the mountains. This single one-hundred-mile-plus narrow pathway was the route used by the locals if they needed to cross the peninsula. This path was most commonly taken by vanilla runners. They would cross the peninsula with big bags of used clothing and return with bags full of extremely valuable vanilla beans they bartered for in the tiny villages.

Surprisingly, the tiny communities we passed through and those we encountered on the other side of the peninsula represented the backbone of the world's vanilla production. These communities grew three crops for the market: vanilla, coffee, and cloves and, strangely enough, had no idea what any of them were used for. The only thing they knew of the outside world was what they saw in videos carried in by entrepreneurs who would bring a generator, screen, and video player and show movies. Most of them were somewhat violent kick-boxing videos from the USA featuring Chuck Norris. Roy bore a strong resemblance to Chuck Norris, and many people ran up to him shouting kickbox—their only English word. We ran into people who believed that the USA bought vanilla to use in making weapons, a sad commentary on a country with a global reputation for war and violent films.

The ridge of mountains ran roughly north and south down the peninsula and marked as good of a center point to our journey as any. The current direction took an unfortunately straight path—straight up and down the mountains. While it was the most direct route, the path had become deeply carved and eroded by rushing water from the nearly constant tropical rains. It had degraded until it was just a narrow groove through the forest about as wide as a fat foot and often nearly knee-deep. I have big calves, and with every step, my muddy and gritty flip-flops would brush against my calf until a rash began to turn into painful cuts. This portion was the most difficult as we tried to straddle the path with one foot on either side of the footworn ditch.

High in the mountains, Roy and I arrived at the remote village of Ampokafo. We got there sooner than expected and stumbled into the community quite suddenly and without warning to them or us. Traveling without a translator, we were always at a disadvantage with even our own porters. In this remote community, something went awry during our initial interactions—whether it was our sudden arrival or something else, we will never know, but my gut feeling is that we somehow frightened someone, most likely by simply showing up.

Naturally, we did not want to frighten or offend anyone and tried to show as best we could that we were sorry and were no threat to anyone. We offered gifts of food and started to move our gear away from the village. We must have succeeded in our apologies because soon, the chief met with our porters and extended gifts of rice to us. I think he was sorry and maybe even embarrassed about the community reaction and, in return, worked hard to let us know we were welcome. He interfered as we pitched camp and had our porters bring everything to the front of his simple home. I assumed they were trying to take our gear but finally got it. He wanted us to stay the night in his home. In all my forest travels through Papua New Guinea, Borneo, Zambia, and more, this had always been one of the taboos. Never sleep in a local home—aside from starting the rumor mill, which would generally humble the biggest gossip you know, there are also issues of cleanliness and pests. Where you have people, you have things that live on people, ranging from bedbugs and botflies to rats, human grime, and more things than you want to imagine in between.

In the end, we gave in and agreed to stay at their home. Among the more harmless of the vivid memories of that stay was seeing a rice winnowing basket on the floor. These were flat reed baskets used for cleaning rice. In this case, it was on the floor and teaming with living, squirming things. There were dozens and dozens of big fat fly maggots. Suspended above it was a dead, flyblown animal that had been found in the forest. When the maggots would fall into the basket, they were collected, cooked, and added to the rice. We actually ended up eating larvae of various insects in our rice during our time there, and if you relied on your taste buds instead of your brain, they were really quite good.

Night came, and Roy and I settled into our sleep sacks on the floor. The house had two rooms. There was a crying baby along with mom and dad in one room, and Roy and I in the living room/kitchen/dining room, maybe fifty or sixty square feet in size. As the family settled down and the candles went out, the room came alive with creatures twittering, rustling, and running here and there. Things ran across us in our sleep sheets, and finally, we began getting lightly nipped here and there. At one point, I sat up and turned on my flashlight. There was a little puff ball of my hair on the floor that had been neatly shorn from my head. The house was alive with rats! After the first couple of nips, Roy and I called it quits, wrapped up our sleep sheets, and snuck outside. But the damage was done. Over the next several days, the little nips festered, and we began to develop unpleasant, oozing sores. Roy's infection was far worse than mine and getting worse every day. His legs, in particular, looked horrible, covered with oozing sores. Staph infections could be quite debilitating. This discomfort combined with strenuous activity sapped our energy and made us doubt we would be able to complete the walk without assistance.

A few more days passed, and we knew we were nearly done. We were no longer doing major hills, and the rushing streams and creeks of the interior disappeared. Instead, we found ourselves plodding alongside a big muddy river moving lazily through the forest. The laziness of the river suggested the ocean was probably not too many days ahead of us. Sick and exhausted, we stumbled through a tiny village—later, we would learn it was Antanambao. The people there were not anxious to see us and either slipped into the forest or into their homes. That was okay. We were not well and did not feel much like making friends, so we just kept going.

Without a real guide or translator, we depended on letting our porters lead us. Finally, a month into our forest transect, we came across a small doubletrack in the forest we knew had been made by a vehicle. It would only be a little further before we could find transportation that would ultimately get us to Antalaha. We had successfully crossed the peninsula, but we had missed our targeted destination of Cap Est by about thirty miles. All in all, missing our destination turned out to be pretty good luck. We were able to get the worst of our sores treated and feel a little better by ending up in a town rather than a simple geographic point.

We were cheerfully greeted, but the very first words I heard in English, "We are so very sorry about your wife," disturbed me. I had been out of touch for a good three weeks and could not imagine what might have happened. Inside, I panicked as my mind raced through dozens of potential scenarios, all of them awful. Spotting my concern, they quickly made it clear that she was okay, but things had not gone as planned.

The story slowly leaked out. Sunni had been left alone in Maroantsetra when we set off on our trek. At the time, we didn't think she needed clear instructions except that a truck would pick her up in the morning and take her to the airport. That part worked fine. A truck arrived and gathered Sunni and her bags and then proceeded around the village collecting people, chickens, rice, and bags until it was packed full, with Sunni jammed in the back against the cab of the truck. First one in, last one out! Hot and stifling, but on their way to the airport.

Once there, the unloading process commenced, and a long wait began. Finally, Sunni heard the words "no plane today." Sunni went back into the truck, followed by the chickens, people, and goats, and did the delivery trip in reverse. This became a daily ritual.

Bad enough, but no one had anticipated that Sunni would be living in Maroantsetra for an additional week or more. There were a few things she was not told about before we left her on her own. The most important was about the lovely woman who came to the house every day to cook. She could only cook if she had money to buy food. The ritual was to leave money in the morning, and the woman would barter for food with her friends and prepare meals. While she clearly cared about Sunni, she cleaned and made what food she could with what was there, but she had no money of her own and could not buy food without cash from Sunni. Without a common language, Sunni did not understand why the meals got smaller and smaller and ultimately disappeared as the days went by. Not that she expected anything for free. She just didn't know the system.

In an attempt to care for herself, she found a little shop that made croissants, something left over from the days of French rule, and in another spot found someone who made homemade yogurt.

Each morning, rain or shine, the truck would come, and the same routine would commence. In the meantime, she missed her international flight home. Back in Los Angeles, her mother had developed the same routine of going to the airport each day to pick up a daughter who never came and never called. Her mom finally panicked and contacted the American embassy. We had filed plans with them, so it was quickly determined where Sunni was, and a small plan was implemented to "rescue" her.

It was too late for me to worry about her, so I worried about myself. We had only been married a short time, and I wasn't sure what her attitude would be when I got home. However, our relationship only grew as she described the entire ordeal as fun, interesting, and refreshing. She read a lot, enjoyed the kids, and would read to curious children who would gather around, fascinated by the strange sounds we know as English. She was never concerned about whether or not someone would come to get her. In fact, whenever the story comes up, Sunni will tell you she was NOT lost. She knew exactly where she was. I can only argue that in the eyes of her mom and anyone else who was expecting her, Sunni WAS lost. It's been a long time, and I'm not sure that Sunni and I agree on how long she was there. I can tell you that when I got home, she was extremely svelte, stretched out, and just plain skinny!

Once stories had been swapped, it was suggested that Roy and I get a couple of days of rest and relaxation at Cap Est. Had we not gotten a bit lost, we would have ended up at *La Résidence Du Cap, Chez George et Magali,* and now we got redirected there and found a couple of sweet little reed and bamboo shacks, a beautiful beach, and a generator, which meant cold beer. There might be a heaven after all!

The proprietor, George, joined me for dinner in a local restaurant. George was probably the most ruggedly and elegantly handsome man I had ever met. Tall, long dark hair and a beard tightly cut French style. Slender but muscular in loose-fitting clothes and enough grease on his hands and arms to suggest he could keep things working around the camp. He was a fascinating South African whose accent changed my name from Bill to Bull. It sounded good coming from him. Here he was in the middle of nowhere with his equally beautiful wife, Magali. Just not what I would have expected.

Surrounded by darkness, the sound of waves, and nothing else, we sat down for dinner. We were seated at a small square table for two with a white linen tablecloth and cloth napkins. The meal was amazing and so strangely out of place. For dessert, George suggested banana flambé. I was not going to argue, so I matched his order. When they came, it was not exactly like what you would expect in a fine French restaurant. The bananas arrived beautifully prepared and splayed out on a lovely dish. The "rum" arrived in a red jerrycan.

George splashed some "fuel" onto his bananas and then passed me the jerrycan. I followed his example and soon we both had flaming plates of browning bananas. After a few moments, George's bonfire dwindled and died out at the perfect time. Inexplicably, my plate bore a strong resemblance to a nuclear holocaust and showed no signs of burning out. As my bananas got darker and darker, I started to take subtle action. George, always the perfect host, showed no sign that anything was amiss. I swished my hand to subdue the flames, but nothing happened. I blew lightly on the bananas, but they continued to burn cheerfully. George continued to chat away. I knew I could put the flames out with one good puff, so I let loose with it. That puff blew fuel and fire all over the white tablecloth. Now there was fire everywhere, and in a bamboo-and-palm-thatched hut, that could have easily spelled disaster. George never missed a beat. Calmly, he took his linen napkin and smothered the fire, and we continued to eat dessert.

George and I were amused when we realized we had mutual friends. We then put it together that we actually had met years before when I was leading a collecting expedition in Zambia. I had inadvertently connected with a rather unsavory character on this expedition. On one evening, we had collected a group of friends for a BBQ in the bush. We now had a common history and a shared passion for where we were in the world. This laid a strong foundation for what would become a special friendship.

Chapter 19

ANTANAMBAO

"A simple life gives birth to more clarity, inner peace,
and meaningful relationships."
~MARGO VADER

A long year passed, but then in 1997, the word came to me through USAID that most of the Masoala Peninsula would be dedicated as the largest tropical park in Madagascar and also be declared a World Heritage site. Seemingly, these two actions would ensure the future of this remarkable place as one of wonder that generations would enjoy. I was asked my opinion about villages within the perimeter of the new park. Once again, entirely unqualified to comment, I spoke from my gut. Madagascar was poor, and these communities in the bush were isolated from the rest of the country and from anything that might seem modern, like running water or electricity. I really felt that if these people were moved from the forest, they would die in the streets. I urged the consortium to let them remain. The decision was made to let them stay, and I was asked to live in Antanambao for periods of time over the next few years. My task was to teach them about butterfly farming and prepare them for the anticipated tourists that would likely follow in the wake of being declared a national park.

As I prepared to return to Madagascar, I regretted that Roy and I had been so tired and sick that we didn't pause to learn more about Antanambao. But we were first and foremost conservation biologists, and people were the enemy. In truth, my eagerness to go back was far less about spending time in Antanambao and more about being in the rainforest, looking for amazing wildlife encounters. Since holding that first snake in my backyard in Poway, I had built my life and career around encounters with wild animals. I think for most people who get interested in conservation, it starts with an animal encounter that is so addictive it causes you to devote your life to finding that next encounter. This also may be the Achilles' heel of conservation—a bunch of people who want to hug endangered wildlife into recovery drive what we do in conservation. Quite unsuspectingly, I was about to learn a new way.

For this first adventure into Antanambao, I would go with only my translator, Tiana. The plan was that four or five weeks later, Sunni would come and join me for the last two weeks of this stay.

As the flight into Madagascar began its long approach, I again noticed the large circles of fire. The rice had been harvested, and now the fields were being burned to help control disease and pests. The fires were lit on a still, fall day and burned out evenly from the center point, creating a series of perfect circles on the landscape. Despite what I knew it was doing to the town's air quality, it was beautiful to see from the air.

The airport was typically chaotic, but I knew the drill now and got through unscathed and headed to Hôtel Colbert for a good night's sleep. The next morning, I headed directly to the office of Project Masoala to get organized and finalize little details.

My contract called for me to be paid per diem. When you lived in a tent and ate white rice at every meal, you could really profit even from a very modest per diem. I was introduced to one of their staff, a local Malagasy man, and we jumped into a brand-new truck and went downtown to get my cash. The Park Masoala was new, money was flowing, and some of the local staff were quite influenced by the new riches in a tragically poor city. As we approached the bank in a desperately congested city, my driver didn't bother searching for a non-existent parking spot but simply drove up onto the sidewalk instead and left me in the passenger seat, waiting. I was too much of an obvious mark. Within moments, a little girl, maybe eight years old, approached the truck and started begging in Malagasy. I just watched her and shrugged my shoulders to let her know I didn't understand her. But she had a set routine and finished in Malagasy no matter what. There was a brief pause, then she launched into it again, this time in French. Again, I shrugged, and again, she went through the whole story. With not so much as a breath, she tried again in German. I was amused until I saw my driver coming. My contract was negotiated in US dollars. The exchange rate was not favorable to the Malagasy ariary, so when my driver came out, he had a roll of cash that required two hands to hold. As he approached the truck, he literally stuck the cash under her nose and then handed the money through the window to me. She was as delighted as I was horror-stricken. She had heard him speak to me in English. As quick as a flash, with a smile as big as tomorrow, she said in perfect English, "Fifty-fifty, mister?" It was a good day for her, not fifty-fifty, but it was a good day.

Tiana and I flew to the small town of Antalaha, where we spent the night. Early the next morning, my friend George from Cap Est was there to meet us. He was our transportation to Cap Est. He warned it would be a long day in a Zodiac inflatable boat on the Indian Ocean. Even so, I was pretty happy, as I was sure it would be easier than walking the nearly thirty miles to Cap Est before dark. As it turned out, I was wrong. A Zodiac does not cut its way through swells. It pounds its way through. On more than one occasion, I was nearly thrown from the boat. Some of this unpleasantness was apparently the fault of the boat's Malagasy pilot. George yelled at him a couple of times and then, after a couple of hours, went to the tiller to take over. My body relaxed as the boat came to a stop, and George moved to the tiller. Our previous pilot was still looking for a seat when George gave it the gas. Actually, he gave it a lot of gas, and the Zodiac leapt forward with amazing speed—EVERYTHING flew. The Malagasy pilot was more than a seaman than I was and managed to fall into his new seat, albeit with a frightened look. Me, I nearly flew out of the boat! What I didn't know was that the irate George wanted to give the pilot a taste of his own medicine, and he did, but he probably should have mentioned it to me. It would be a long eight hours in rough seas. Suddenly, a nice little two-day walk through the forest did not seem too bad by comparison.

It was great to be back at Cap Est. It was all the wonderful things I remembered and maybe more. A simple but cozy bungalow, a cold beer, and a shower. It just could not get better than this. Tiana, George, and I planned our next day over a nice fish dinner and a big side dish of white rice. We would have to leave just after dawn to make it to Antanambao before dark and safely set up our tents. George offered a "shortcut" through the littoral swamp, but it didn't sound right to go through a swamp. I had learned from hard experience that shortcuts were seldom actually shortcuts. Maybe some other day.

After "losing" Sunni in Maroantsetra in 1995, my bosses at the zoo were concerned about me being out of touch for so long and equally concerned that Sunni would travel by herself to meet me in the rainforest. They decided I should carry a satellite phone I could use in an emergency, and that when Sunni came, she would travel with an escort from the zoo. The satellite phone might seem like no big deal, but in 1997, it was over thirty pounds of additional gear, mostly big batteries. By the time Tiana and I packed up enough rice for several weeks, our tents, the phone, and batteries along with other miscellaneous gear, it was clear we would either have to make a couple of trips or hire some help. Help seemed the smart way to go, so with a couple of porters, we set off the next morning just before dawn.

Minus the humidity, heat, and terribly muddy path, the route to Antanambao from this side of the peninsula was not bad. There were a few tiny villages of maybe a hundred people in each and then mostly forest and some grazing land for the zebu cows. Lemurs could be spotted along with spectacular birds like the blue coua. As usual, there were lots of little streams to cross. I didn't mind wading across, but every once in a while, there would be a narrow log spanning the water. It was absolutely necessary to balance on that with your bags and walk across. I have a terrible sense of balance and generally had to crawl across these logs. After all, wading is one kind of wet, and falling in is another.

It was late in the afternoon when our small team of porters, Tiana, and I arrived in Antanambao. We hurried to set our tents up in the tiny village. Someone came and spoke quietly but urgently to Tiana. The only word I caught was "vazaha," their term for a traveler, so I knew the conversation was about me. I heard the word vazaha often, but never in association with a Malagasy person—it seemed to me to be reserved for Caucasians. Before long, we were packing again. Tiana had been told in no uncertain terms vazaha could not stay in the village. Not wanting to cause a ruckus on day one, we quickly packed up and headed a little way upstream, where we set up camp.

Next on the list was setting up for meals and finding a place to bathe. If not for the satellite phone, we were at least three days from the nearest phone and another day from decent medical facilities. Because of this, our health and safety were always an extremely high priority. Our bath, right next to our camp, was the Iagnobe River. It was rumored there were crocodiles in the river. While we wanted to be clean, we also didn't want to be eaten right off the bat. Tiana watched and saw where everyone was going to bathe and do their dishes. We waited politely and, as they all left and went back to the village, went to bathe. But before we were in the water, we heard what I learned would be a frequent message—vazaha cannot bathe there. We moved somewhat upstream, where a small group of zebu cows was drinking, and bathed with them. We hoped that if there were crocodiles, they would prefer zebu to the tough old vazaha.

I am a pretty quick learner, and it became clear we were not going to have success in a community where no one trusted us. We were able to have meals in the village with a beautiful couple, Jean Luc and Marie Ange. It took me a long time to figure out they were not from Antanambao and worked for Project Masoala, which explained why, unlike everyone else in the village, they were kind to us.

Everyone else in this tiny community was at least distrustful and, at worse, terrified. If I accidentally surprised a child out on a walk, it was likely their terror would be absolute. Trying to keep an eye on me and run full tilt away led to awful falls and collisions. I really thought someone might get injured because of me.

We were going to need a lot more than the friendship of Jean Luc and Marie Ange to make our time there worthwhile. As the days passed and the third week began, we seemed to be making no progress at all. I finally called it off, and we started to pack up our camp. Perhaps this was finally the time when my enthusiasm would not be enough to replace a basic lack of skills. It really should have been an anthropologist doing this, not a biologist who wasn't sure he liked these people any more than they liked him. As we were packing, I spotted a little boy hiding under the bushes, watching us. No more than eighteen months old, he was probably too young to know I might eat him. I stopped what I was doing and turned my back to him to avoid frightening him away. Then I counted to five in Malagasy and then in English: araiky, aroa, telo, efatra, dimy. One, two, three, four, five. Over and over for several minutes with no reply. Finally, I slowly turned so we could make eye contact and continued counting, leaving little gaps, hoping he would chime in. After a short eternity, he began to count. Slowly and with a real accent, but we were relating. Our tents remained set up, and we settled back in. Thanks to this little boy, we were going to stay.

Over the next few days, I learned his name was Emilien. He continued to come and visit. Soon he brought friends, and together, we sang songs, took pictures, and shared food. Ultimately, their moms came to see what we were doing, and I could feel a thaw begin. One evening, around the fire with Tiana translating for me, I asked why the children were so terrified and the adults so distrustful. They said there were terrible things at play. Some people in the community believed I had come to steal children, but even more whispered that vazaha would eat children and steal the spirits of adults.

Sunni was coming for a visit, and as anxious as I was to see her, I feared it was too soon. I was worried about her arrival in Antanambao because Tiana and I were finally being accepted. Adding Sunni to the social mix could easily be a setback. But even with the satellite phone for communication, it was too late. Sunni had begun the seven-day trip to get here, and we would have to deal with it. Sunni would arrive sometime around her birthday on November 20, give or take a few days in either direction, so I taught the kids to sing happy birthday and tried to make it Tiana's responsibility to prepare the community for her arrival. I had to leave in the wee hours to make it out to the coast to meet her boat.

There were so many steps in her journey and so many places where it would be easy to miss a connection. Our initial plans were for George to meet Sunni in Antananarivo when she arrived from Los Angeles. At the last minute, George's dad fell ill, and George had to go to South Africa. This had the potential to really complicate things. As we brainstormed how to sort this out, I realized George would leave Antananarivo at roughly the same time Sunni would be arriving. It seemed like there was a remote chance they would cross paths, and George could share critical instructions with her. The problem was, they had never met and didn't know what each other looked like. As small as the airport was by global standards, it was still a busy international airport. The odds were against us. I managed to shoot an email to Sunni, not knowing if it would get to her. The message was simple. "When you arrive in Madagascar, look for the most handsome man in the airport and ask him if he is George."

Uncertain if she would find George and more uncertain about all the connections she needed to make, I could only ballpark when she would arrive. I left Antanambao before dawn and walked all day. I arrived at the coast as the light was fading. I had just enough time to set up my tent, boil up some rice, and settle in for the night.

For the next several days, I spent my time scanning the ocean with my binoculars, looking for a Zodiac raft, a skiff, or any kind of boat capable of making the journey from Antalaha. As days slid by, I became more and more anxious. Finally, on the horizon, a little speck of something was headed my way. I parked on the beach and watched as the boat slowly took shape. I could tell it was on a beeline for where I was. It had to be Sunni. No one else had any reason to be here. I was excited beyond words and relieved she had made it. We were madly in love, and I had missed her. I could not wait to hold her in my arms. I waded out waist-deep, waiting for the boat to draw near. I knew she had to be as anxious and excited as I was. Then the boat stopped. It was a couple of hundred yards out and too small to need to anchor that far from shore. I scanned it with my binoculars and could make out a few men and a woman I knew had to be Sunni, but not much else. After what seemed like an eternity, the boat finally made its approach to shore. As it turned out, Sunni was an avid fisherman and hooked into something big. There was no way she was not going to land that fish; we could hug after the battle was over.

We enjoyed a sweet reunion on a quiet beach, listening to the small waves break onto the shore just outside our camp. We had a lot to catch up on, but my biggest concern was her connections. I asked, "Did you find George?" Her face lit up. "Are you kidding? How could I miss him!" Early the next morning, we set out for

Antanambao. I spent the long walk briefing Sunni on community politics and our slow integration into the community. I remained worried about how Sunni would be greeted.

It was late when we finally finished our walk and strolled into Antanambao. Immediately, a woman from my group of butterfly farmer trainees approached. She greeted Sunni with a warm smile and a kiss on each cheek, then without hesitation, she felt Sunni's breasts. Then the other women arrived; there was lots of giggling and kisses, and they all fondled Sunni's breasts. I felt like I had been left out of the important tradition of feeling a woman's breasts when I was introduced. Sunni smiled and laughed and allowed the process to go on. Then Tiana arrived, and light was slowly shed on this special behavior.

In Antanambao, women had children "when they are tall enough." Generally, this meant they were quite young. They rarely wore a brassiere and never one that was properly fitted. They nursed baby after baby, sometimes more on one side than the other. By the time they were in their twenties, it was fair to say their breasts had been through a lot! Sunni would celebrate her forty-fourth birthday in Antanambao. She had never had children and pretty much always wore a fitted bra. She had great breasts, and now everyone was appreciating that fact.

With Tiana there to help, we began a conversation about breasts and babies that got off to a rocky start. Sunni explained to Tiana, "I have never had babies and have always worn a bra." Immediately, all eyes left Sunni and locked on me. It took a moment for me to understand, but then I got it. They saw me as unable to perform my manly obligations. I could not sit still for that! Quickly, I explained it was intentional and that we used birth control. This opened a whole new can of worms. These women wanted to have babies, but not all the time. The idea that they could possibly have a choice in the matter was overwhelming. What we found time and time again was women had babies because they had no choice in the matter. One of the best reasons to raise people out of poverty is the idea that we could better manage population growth on our planet with a little education. Without my knowing it, a seed was planted in my mind.

Although separated by a week at home, it turned out that Sunni's birthday and Thanksgiving were going to share a day in Antanambao. Throughout the trek of 1995 and my time thus far in Antanambao, all I had ever eaten was white rice. Occasionally, dried insect larvae or fish were crumbled over the top, but that was it. On Sunni's birthday, the village transformed itself. Woven mats were laid out on the pathway the entire length of the village, and piles of cooked rice were dumped every few feet. They had made bread, killed chickens, and even a cow. Little kids sang a discordant Hoppy Burfday, and the party began.

Tiana had shared that Thanksgiving was about thankfulness and that it would make us feel at home. We were touched deeply. Though I had thought I had penetrated the social barriers and been accepted into the village, I had only begun the process. Sunni's arrival painted a more complete picture of me, which really allowed us to be part of their community.

The kids were always the center of life in the community. They worked hard from an early age, but it was a game to them. Catching tiny minnows and aquatic larva to dry and sprinkle on their rice. Helping in the rice fields or cleaning cloves. There was always something for them to do. One beautiful little girl named Julia attached herself to Sunni. She was wonderfully photogenic, and each year, we took her picture as she grew ever more beautiful.

For the next three years, for several months of each year, this would be our life, working and loving with the poorest, happiest, and most generous people you could ever imagine. Through it all, Emilien was always there. He rode on my feet, or I would carry him on my shoulders, but he was my constant companion during our frequent stays in Antanambao.

Emilien was always there. On my lap, on my shoulders,
or standing on my feet. We were inseparable.

Chapter 20

SAYING GOODBYE

"Everything has to come to an end, sometime."
~L. FRANK BAUM

In November of 1999, our contract to work in Madagascar and be part of this remarkable community was scheduled to end. I had ultimately survived the infamous centipede attack on my face with the primary damage being to my ego. We had done our job, and now, like so many other times in life, it was time to start the next project—to walk away from this one and make room for the next one.

Sunni and I woke early; there was a lot to do. This would be our last day in Antanambao. We sat over a bowl of rice and talked about what an amazing experience it had been and, of course, wondered if we would ever come back. Almost five years earlier, Roy and I had trudged through the mud, tired and unhappy. Kids had fled into the forest, and the few adults that remained nearby had simply glared at us. My reception eighteen months later had not been much warmer, in fact, maybe even more tepid. Over time, sweet little Emilien had changed all that. We had come to know his friends and family, and through that, we joined a remarkable community.

He had grown a lot in just a few years, from sitting on our hips and shoulders to standing on our feet as we walked about. If we stopped and sat, he was there, sitting next to us or standing between our legs. He would occasionally chase a chicken with the other kids until he was out of sight, but it was rare for him to be more than a shout away. We knew today would be awful because it simply had to be. We had gone from strangers to residents, from residents to friends. Real friends, the kind you made when words were never the first way you communicated. We had talked about everything, and I believed they spoke English while they believed I spoke Malagasy—of course, neither was true, it just seemed that way. Deep into a conversation, we would suddenly realize we had no idea what the other was saying. We would laugh hard and call out for Tiana to save us. The words "Ah, Tiana" had become a regular echo in the village as either Sunni or I would need her help. We had celebrated the births of babies, mourned people passing, and attended Trombas, where we spoke with the dead. We were all too aware that Madagascar was antipodal, both geographically and socially, from our home. Chances were all too good that we would never be back.

There was a lot of preparation before we could go. Porters would leave by late morning, carrying most of the gear we had from our repeated visits. We were left with our tents and small day packs with things we would need on the way out.

We tried hard to treat it like any other day. Sunni sat with the women and cleaned freshly picked cloves of nutmeg while I helped Jean Luc work silently in the garden. There was time for reflection about our time in this different and special place. Some things had changed because we came. There was the Vazaha Bridge, a long footbridge where none had existed before, and there was a Vazaha Toilet and a butterfly garden next to Jean Luc's thriving nursery. But after several years, that was all there was, and that was good. Our goal had not been to change their way of life, but to protect it to whatever degree they might want. Soon there would be hikers and tourists, and this secret place would be known to the world. We could only hope the world would be kind to them.

The thirty-five-pound satellite phone was packed up and handed off to the porters, as were a variety of other things we would not need for our last few hours in the field. They set off at a fast trot. They would make short work of the trip to Antalaha while Sunni and I would need a couple of days.

After lunch, we sat under the lychee trees snacking on their sweet fruit and watched the ladies doing their hair. I always loved watching this and was never made to feel like a voyeur. Though not shy, it was not typical for the women to go around topless unless they were down at the river doing laundry or, occasionally, while getting their hair done. The blazing heat of the peninsula made it easier to wear their hair tightly braided and close to their heads, so there was only an hour or so every few days when they would undo their braids and wash their hair. On that day, they would team up with a girlfriend, lay a woven mat on the dirt under a tree, and lie down to do each other's hair. I was surprised at how long their hair was and how different they were with it down. They looked beautiful in the warm sun, their golden skin shining in the sunlight. For those brief moments, these women, who lived such difficult lives by our standards and worked so hard by any standard, would appear to live in Eden.

The afternoon grew increasingly hot. It was a relief to think this would be the last nap in this blistering hot, sweaty, tropical oven. The heat came, and Tiana went to her tent, Sunni to hers, and me to mine. I went through the ritual of setting my water bottle to the right side of my pillow and my flashlight to the left. I folded up my toilet paper fan and zipped up my tent tightly. As the afternoon darkened, we all drifted off into our separate slumbers and dreams.

In the fading twilight, I heard Tiana begin to rustle around. It was time to get up and help with dinner. I pulled on my clothes and, with my flashlight in hand, rolled out of the tent about the same moment Sunni did. The three of us simultaneously took on expressions of bewilderment. Where normally the village would be active with many cooking fires, tonight was different. The village was dark, and there appeared to be no one there. Instead of several fires, there was only one and no one in sight. We did the only thing we could think to do and went and sat next to the fire.

The firelight made the surrounding village and forest seem even darker than they really were. The three of us chatted, drank ronomo-pong, and waited. Finally, we heard some sounds from the darkness that seemed random, just thumps from the distance. Then those thumps fell into a pattern, and the sound came from all sides; it was the rhythmic stomping of feet. It grew closer and louder, and then familiar voices chimed in with chanting and song. We could not see them out in the dark, but we knew in a flash the whole village, all two hundred of them, were singing and dancing outside the circle of fire. It was both beautiful and mystifying until one person stepped into the light, bearing a small gift for Sunni and me. Then another person, and another. A clove, a flower, a leaf, a vanilla bean, a shell. It hit me like a lightning bolt. They were thanking us and saying goodbye. We burst into an uncontrollable flow of tears. These people from this little place with no running water or power, where everyone wore used clothing acquired by trading cloves, coffee, and vanilla, were stepping into the firelight to give the richest people on earth a gift.

It went on all evening. Hugs, gifts, and then the next person would repeat the ritual. We were drained emotionally and physically by the impact of the evening. As remarkably wonderful as it was, we did not want to do anything like it again in the morning. We did not have it in us to say goodbye again, to any of them—least of all,

Emilien. We knew we needed a private and quiet departure. After a quick chat with Tiana, we agreed she would leave before dawn and make a beeline for the coast to make arrangements for our exit. Sunni and I would follow at first light with our last few belongings, and hopefully, all of us would be gone before the village woke up in the morning. Drained, dehydrated, and exhausted, we fell into our tents and slept deeply.

We never suspected the tears and difficult conversations taking place in a tiny reed house just a few doors away from where we slept. Emilien was with his mom and dad. His dad was stern, and his mom was crying. At the same time, everything Emilien owned was being put neatly into one tiny bag. At four years old, he could not fully grasp the conversation and why his dad—a man with a perpetual smile—was so stern or why his loving mom was so frightened. His sleepy eyes closed. Tomorrow would be a new day.

It seemed like I had just closed my eyes when I heard Tiana drop her tent, pack up, and leave Antanambao. I dozed off again until just before dawn. I lay on my back in my sleep sack and listened to the moisture dripping from the trees for the last time. Everything inside me fought the decision to get up and leave, but the demands of timing and a world that would not wait for us made the decision for me. It would not get easier, so we might as well get it over with. I crawled out and woke Sunni. We folded up our tents as quickly and quietly as we could. The dawn had just broken when we completed our packing and wordlessly began to creep away.

Only a few steps away from our now vacant campsite, we were stopped by three people. First, there was Emilien's dad. Even in the low light, he was a handsome man, slender with beautiful teeth and a broad, white smile. Almost as a counterpoint, Emilen's mom stood shorter and slightly stockier, with an expression that said the weight of the world was on her shoulders. Between them was a bewildered little Emilien with a frightened smile and dressed in the nicest clothes we had ever seen him in. Our Malagasy was bad, but his little bag of clothes and his mom's look told us all we needed to know. They were giving us their son. Giving us their cherished, bold little boy to go somewhere they could not even imagine. It was a lot to take in. Tiana was gone, so all the communication was through looks, gestures, and the painfully few words we had picked up in our time there. As Sunni and I processed the information, we knew immediately we could not take him. No one outside of this little village knew of Emilien's existence. There was no way he could leave the country, and there was nothing we could do. Worse yet, there was nothing we could say. Without words, we cried with tears we thought had been spent, hugged them, and then simply walked away.

Five months later, a tropical disturbance formed in the Australian cyclone basin. It moved north and west until it entered the Indian cyclone basin. Finally, an eye formed, and on March 27, 2000, tropical cyclone Hudah was officially born. By April 1, this storm was designated as an intense tropical cyclone. On the evening of April 2, with wind gusts of 145 mph, it crashed into Madagascar just southeast of Antalaha. The only thing southeast of Antalaha was Cap Est and Antanambao. Twenty-five-foot waves crashed on the shores of the peninsula, where George and Magali had their beachfront ecotourism lodge.

Unaware of the advancing cyclone, George had left Magali and their tiny son, Matthew, while he made a trip to Antananarivo. By the time he learned of the cyclone, there was nothing he could do. He was on the radio with Magali until late afternoon when the arriving storm took out all communications. All he could do was wait. Magali was now alone in the dark with a tiny son, a Peace Corps volunteer, and nothing else.

Though almost everything in Cap Est was made of sticks, bamboo, and reeds, George had been picky about the kitchen that would serve their guests. The floor of the kitchen had been made of concrete, so he could keep it clean. When the kitchen was finished, there was concrete left over. This far out, nothing was wasted. There was not a

Dressed in his very best clothing and with everything else he owned packed into a woven bag, Emilien was presented to us to take to the USA. This moment would ultimately cause me to rethink all I had done in conservation work.

lot, but enough to do the walls of their bathroom in their bungalow. Their lodge and all its bungalows were gone within moments, but it would take a bit longer for the house to go—it was set back from the beach and a bit more protected. Sadly, though, there would be no real protection from this storm. The storm blotted out any light from the sky. In pitch darkness, the roof disappeared in a loud crash embraced before and after by deafening claps of thunder. Moments later, the walls began to break apart, each piece taking off like reckless kites in the high wind.

Magali, Matthew, and the Peace Corps volunteer retreated together into the last structure, the bathroom, tasting only the saltwater blown into their faces. The bathroom door exploded off its hinges and disappeared into the night, leaving them exposed and vulnerable. There was nowhere left to go. All Magali could do was use her body to shield her terrified son. The Peace Corps volunteer huddled with them. Whether by divine plan or accident, the ferocious winds picked up a mattress and blew it solidly against the doorway of the bathroom. There it stayed, blocking the wind and water. It probably saved their lives. Only when the storm finally passed and daylight peeked through the cracks did Magali have the nerve to push the mattress away. As far as she could see in every direction, there was destruction and nothing else—not a single standing structure or undamaged tree. The three of them were truly alone, with nothing in the middle of nowhere.

Chapter 21

RESCUES THWARTED

"Reaching out to rescue one another under any condition
is an eternal measure of love."
~RONALD A. RASBAND

For more than one hundred miles, every man-made structure was destroyed. The runway in Antalaha was rendered unusable, and one hundred people (likely more) up and down the peninsula lost their lives. Village huts were built on short stilts. As roofs and walls disappeared in the raging winds, people sought shelter under their homes, only to be drowned or forced out by rising waters.

It was a difficult night for George in Antananarivo. With no way of getting news, he was frantic and in a state of emotional despair. All his strengths and talents could not solve this problem. As soon as a pilot was willing to make the flight to Antalaha, George urged them into the air. As they neared Antalaha and the closest airport to Cap Est and his family, the devastation of the cyclone became clear. Antalaha was a good fifty miles from Magali and where the storm had made direct landfall, yet even here, there was total destruction for as far as George could see. One flyover and the pilot informed George they could not land. The damage to the commercial runway and debris scattered about made a landing too dangerous.

I remembered not too many years earlier seeing George's anger explode when the pilot of our Zodiac boat didn't perform to his standards. It was noteworthy and nearly got me drowned, but he taught the pilot a lesson. I could easily imagine George's reaction when the pilot told him they couldn't land. Long story short, the plane landed safely in Antalaha.

George was now in Antalaha, but still had no path to search for his family. An able boatman, he tried to get a boat, knowing that under the best of conditions, it would be an eight-hour ride on the Indian Ocean, and these were clearly not the best of conditions. The seas were high and loaded with debris. After a careful reconnaissance, a boat was ruled out. Hopeful that a motorbike would be able to navigate the forest paths, George again set out, but the paths were no longer there. The rainforest that had been there before had been transformed into a jungle in the truest sense of the word. Twisted, broken, and uprooted trees blocked his every turn. In deep despair, George gave up. He was crushed, his heart broken, and suddenly, he knew he did not want to get to the barren site that was once *La Résidence du Cap; Chez George et Magali.*

With all options exhausted, George pleaded with a local non-profit that had helicoptered into Antalaha to help. He was able to get them to search Cap Est while he waited at the airport for news.

For Magali, the appearance of a helicopter was quite unexpected. In this place, you couldn't expect help from outside; you took care of yourself. But its appearance was as welcome as it was unexpected. For her and her son, safety was at hand.

Once back in Antalaha, George's family was once again intact, but sadly, George was not and would never be again. The following years were difficult. Shortly after the cyclone, George and I visited Cap Est. He was broken. I watched him take a bottle cap, fill it with honey, and place it on the ground in the middle of the wreckage. Our eyes met. Mine had an unspoken question. George answered, "The bees. It's for the bees. There is nothing left for them."

George struggled emotionally. It was as though his space in the world had been destroyed, along with his dream of raising a family in the next best thing to the mythical Garden of Eden. We collaborated briefly about rebuilding schools near Antalaha, but ultimately, he took a job with USAID. I think he did this to get as far away from the lost hopes and memories as he possibly could. He took his family to Sudan. There, Magali couldn't leave the compound or drive a car. To make matters worse, George isolated himself from Magali and Matthew. He buried himself in his work, but the pain and anger inside of him continued to burn. The strains on the family were too much. Magali returned to Madagascar with her son, where she hoped she could resettle and find some sense of normalcy.

Among George's friends was our connection from Zambia, that bad penny that always seemed to pop in and out of George's life at critical moments. Rory was edgy and rarely involved in things that were entirely legal. Sometime in all of this, he contacted George and took advantage of his frustrations. Rory provided an opportunity for George to go even further from home, teased by an offer of good money. George took employment with the Security Institute and deployed to Afghanistan. There he assisted in transporting military VIPs in and out of various military hot spots. On one such assignment in 2006, a helicopter he was in was shot down. George was killed, along with everyone else on board.

Immediately after the storm, Sunni and I appealed to the zoo and to other organizations that had supported the work in Madagascar for funds to search for Emilien and help where we could. Each one told us no. Conservation funds were to save animals and habitats. This was a human crisis. It was now clear that the two issues would never meet. A dear friend made a contribution through the zoo to help. With those funds and our personal money, we made a trip to the peninsula to search for our friends.

One of our first stops was the ruins of Cap Est. Magali was expecting us and had hiked partway to Antalaha to meet us. It had been a year since we had seen her. She looked thin and tired but happy to see us. We sat at the side of the trail, resting and catching up. She talked with Sunni about the night of the cyclone. I turned on the video camera to catch her voice as she spoke. Sunni and I had received our first reports of the disaster by email and could now see the impact firsthand and hear a firsthand account of the terror the storm brought. The forest, along with their tiny tropical lodge, had clearly been obliterated by the storm. The lodge was the most carefully constructed facility in this part of the peninsula. Its destruction told us volumes about the impact it likely had on our little village and the families there. For the last eight or nine miles of our journey, not a single tree over ten feet tall had its branches. For as far as we could see, it looked as though a giant chainsaw had been taken to the forest. Portions of the hot, dry forest now burned with flames leaping thirty feet into the air. What had once been a rainforest trail now baked under a broiling tropical sun. We turned off the trail and toward Résidence du Cap, and the first sight was the remains of their home, the roof and nearly all the walls ripped away. Where beautiful bungalows once stood was bare sand. The storm took everything—even the debris.

I am not sure how many times Magali had brought friends here and how many times they had stood where so much had been invested and lost. But today, Magali had to do it again. Then we connected with George—I didn't realize it would be the last time I would see him.

We had no translator, porters, or help of any kind. People were taking shelter under black tarps dropped from helicopters by

USAID. Each time we asked about Emilien, we were sent in another direction and, in each case, to funerals. A ragged little girl covered in open sores and missing all her hair tugged at Sunni's arm. I didn't recognize her, but Sunni assured me it was our beautiful and outgoing Julia. Basically, we were lost, out of time and out of money. We had no translator to help us communicate and share our thoughts. Once again, the only thing we could do was the most painful and something we had done far too often. We had to walk away.

Chapter 22

On the WINGS *of the* CONDOR, *the Birth of* ECOLIFE

"Education is what remains after one has forgotten
what one has learned in school."

~UNKNOWN

After years of hard work in Mexico to protect the monarch butterfly, hundreds of millions of butterflies died in one night. After years of dangerous work to expose graft and corruption in the program in Paraguay, the program was again embraced. The conservation community at large, my community, demonstrated they could walk away from a little boy—in fact, an entire community—because they were not wild animals or plants.

So it was that in the first few years of a new millennium (2000 to 2003), I was slapped into conservation sobriety. My lessons were hard-earned. After years of dedicated and collaborative conservation work in Mexico, our traditional tools had made no measurable impact on the conservation of the monarch butterfly. To be honest, the monarch butterfly faced many threats in addition to those in the Mexican forest, but on that one front, our work proved to be as meaningless as any other being done anywhere in the monarch's range. Paraguay had demonstrated the horrific side of humanity I had been able to quietly ignore for most of my life, from bigotry to corruption and worse. But the last straw was Madagascar. Now the conservation community I had dedicated my professional life to showed that not only was it largely without impact, subject to horrific corruption, but now I knew that conservation was willing to turn its back on people, preferring to turn them into environmental refugees.

I had tried to change the zoo by launching the Applied Conservation Division, which would allow the tremendous reach of the Zoological Society to truly embrace measurable conservation, and I had failed. I had tried to solve horrific issues of bigotry and lawlessness in Paraguay, and I had failed. I had seen the coldness of heart from my own conservation community, from those that turned their backs on condors to protect their jobs to those who turned their backs on entire populations of people around the world in the interest of single species protectionism.

I had more than once told my colleagues that the last thing the world needed was another nonprofit group. Particularly another one focused on conserving wildlife. It had always seemed to me that everyone had a pet project that no one could do better than they could, so they created another nonprofit. Suddenly, I found myself prepared to go down that path. At forty-eight years old, I needed to change and find a new job, a new organization, and a new mission, but in the short term, I needed to step back and think.

While I was curator of birds for the zoo and interviewing prospective new keepers, the one thing I did not want to hear from them was, "I just love animals so much." Strangely, that was my panic button. Running a zoo is a business. Animals are bought and sold and, even within the zoo, are moved around to the best advantage of the zoo. They get sick; some are euthanized—unlike your pet, there are cases where the decision is simply a financial one. When you work with live animals, it becomes inevitable that you will deal with dead animals. A keeper that "loves" animals was likely to be a big problem at some point.

At the same time, there was that little voice saying, you got into this because YOU love animals. My most treasured photos are of me holding Jim, the gorilla, or baby cheetahs play-mauling me. That baby chicken in 1961 that set my career path caught my attention because it was cute and fluffy. My sophisticated education could not erase that part of me. My early success in the condor program was because I was good at handling birds. Really my career in conservation was predicated on a desire to be around animals. Maybe this was part of the problem in conservation, that for many of us, the initial impetus was simply a love of animals. How much had this passion for animals tainted my approach? It was time to really back up, take away as many personal biases as possible, and rethink my life, what I was doing, and how I would move forward.

I strongly maintain that we humans are much simpler than we think, and our motivations are far less different from other forms of life. Like every other species, we eat, drink, and breathe so we can reproduce. It is that simple. Our jealousy drives us to guard our mates so that we don't end up raising someone else's babies. We love so we can create stability, which increases the survival and success of our offspring. While some birds use spectacular plumage to attract mates, others must build elaborate courtship structures like bowers. People courtship feed our mates just like so many animals, and we do courtship dances and other elaborate rituals. So maybe everything we do is ultimately about our future and that of the children we are so determined to create.

Immediately, people who understand conservation will say I am dead wrong—we are clearly working very hard at killing ourselves. Let's talk about some basic behavioral science. We respond to a variety of stimuli in largely predictable ways. We sense when we run out of oxygen in our bloodstream and take a breath. In a proximate way, we breathe because we have run out of oxygen, but ultimately, we breathe for the larger purpose of staying alive (and reproducing). We have sex because it feels good; that is the proximate cause. Ultimately, we have sex to have babies. I will maintain that most of our bad short-term behaviors are proximate (read that as shortsighted) reactions that end up confounding our ultimate goal of survival. I cut a tree down today because I need a place to live. Tomorrow, when I run out of air, I might well wish I had not cut the tree down, even though it seemed like a good idea at the time. We react in very proximate ways that have an evolutionary advantage in a natural world, but we have changed that world and brought our population to unprecedented numbers. Now, these shortsighted reactions ultimately threaten our future on this planet.

Where have we gone wrong, and what, in fact, is the greatest threat to animals, our resources, and our future? Let's zoom way out. Abandon for the moment our love of animals and each other. Let's examine the earth as extraterrestrials—or forgive me, curators. How would we save this complicated, interrelated collection of life? Start by asking yourself what the most common cause of extinction is and force yourself to think long-term, big picture. Go past saving a bird and ask about saving the diverse world of species. Perhaps one of the best references for an overall look is the Red Data Books maintained by the International Union for Conservation of Nature (IUCN). They work hard to list all the threatened and endangered species on the planet and the causes for their decline. Scanning through this horrific list, I was immediately struck by one thing. Overwhelmingly, species are going extinct because their homes are destroyed or converted to other uses. So it is logical to ask: what are the primary drivers of habitat loss? That data is also easily accessible. Today, habitat loss is overwhelmingly driven by two related processes: conversion of open spaces to agriculture and climate change. I describe these as closely related because a primary force behind climate change is industrialized agriculture. Rarely do you see a species poached or hunted to extinction. We are simply destroying their homes so we can eat.

To explain this, let's use African elephants as an example. It is likely that sometime during the next forty years, animals like elephants and rhinoceros will disappear forever. All you need to do is google them to see that poaching will nail the lid to their coffin tightly shut. But ultimately, poaching only matters because their populations have been so badly reduced by habitat loss. Known rates of poaching cannot and do not entirely account for the dramatic decline in their numbers. According to the World Wildlife Fund, there were as many as ten million African elephants in the 1930s. Using that as a starting point, we can make some assumptions. We know, within a margin of error, what the average population growth is in a healthy population. Without taking you through all the rigorous math, if we take their growth rate and the current and historic poaching rates, there should still be millions of elephants. Poaching rates are not high enough to fully account for their decline. While nonprofits are screaming for funds to stop poaching, African countries like Botswana are culling elephants and are doing it because there is no place left for the elephants to live. The habitats they survived in are largely gone—largely converted to agriculture. If you want to find out why elephants are really in trouble, just open another bottle of Tusker beer while in Kenya and look out across the barley fields that used to be home to

So many of us get into conservation because of a passion for wildlife.
It is a hard lesson to let go of the animals and embrace human
behavior in order to save a butterfly.

elephants. Admittedly, I am picking on Tusker because of its name. It is not just growing barley that kills off elephants and other wildlife; it is agriculture in general. This suggests that if we really care about wildlife, we have to do something about the way we farm and the way we eat.

Right behind agriculture, and again related to how we eat, I found another important impact on habitats and endangered species that surprised me. A staggering three billion impoverished people cook over an open fire, most often inside their homes. Imagine the environmental impact of three billion people cutting firewood out of disappearing forests every day around the world. If we assume a family size of five, that is six hundred million families harvesting wood to cook. It is not unusual for each of these fires to consume twenty or more trees per year per family. That is twelve billion trees cut annually to cook food. Twelve billion trees that no longer sequester carbon, but in fact, are being converted into CO_2 and dumped into our atmosphere. And the story doesn't end here. It turns out that illnesses and diseases associated with inhaling the smoke from these fires are the single biggest killer of people in the world! The total number of global deaths associated with dirty drinking water, malaria, breast cancer, and AIDS is still fewer people than the 4.3 million deaths the World Health Organization estimates are caused by indoor air pollution.

The remarkable thing about these two big items driving extinction is that humans will be the most direct beneficiary of changing our behavior and protecting habitats.

With these two issues alone, we have a conservation crisis on a nearly unimaginable scale. While doing something about it may well be the most important step on the planet, it is an empty bucket for most conservationists. Where are the animals we so dearly desire to embrace with our work? Conservationists are not trained as farmers, nor are they trained in humanitarian efforts. We are too focused on saving a tree, a condor, and an elephant, all the while failing to see or address the core causes of their decline. In the years spent on artificially reversing the population trend in the California condor, hundreds if not thousands of other species disappeared, and many more were brought closer to the brink of extinction. In my lifetime, the golden toad from Costa Rica, the dusky seaside sparrow of Florida, the St. Croix racer snake, and hundreds of others are gone. IUCN estimated that in the 2010s, we lost an average of sixteen known species annually. We know we can raise money to defeat poachers because it makes for sexy marketing, but can we find the same funding and zeal and apply it to programs that will really make a difference? Can we find funds for sustainable agriculture to ensure a home for animals? Can we improve people's lives and lift them from poverty enough that they don't need to cut twelve billion trees down for firewood?

During my career, I made conscious decisions to walk away from the California condor program and Paraguay. Ultimately, I walked away from a little boy and his community in Madagascar. There must be better ways to do this work. By clearly defining the real problems, I believe we can create an environmental nonprofit and a path forward that would have meaningful, measurable, and profound impacts. One where I would never need to walk away from a small child again.

Turns out, *I know we can.* That belief, along with the brutal lessons of Madagascar, monarchs in Mexico, and the Paraguay fiasco, led me to believe there was room in the world for at least one more conservation NGO, but one that would need to be very different from all the others. My friends and I all brainstormed. We argued until late into the night about the best approaches, and these arguments led me to conservation strategies I had never imagined. I was slow coming around to it, but I remembered the charcoal edits to the El Cementerio sign in El Rosario, and the firewood issue clicked. Finally, my good friend, Eric Hallstein, an up-and-coming business consultant, and I sat down and put together the bones and paperwork for ECOLIFE Conservation. We decided to see if data and sound marketing could move the needle and maybe save the world. In 2003, ECOLIFE Conservation was officially recognized as yet another conservation nonprofit, but different from all the others. By striking at the cause of the problems and focusing on the benefits to people, we are unique in the field.

Chapter 23

EARLY STRUGGLES

"A best friend is the only one that walks into your life
when the world has walked out."

~SHANNON L. ALDER

ECOLIFE struggled. We didn't know that most successful nonprofits were launched with huge pre-arranged support. We simply believed in what we knew and were sure others would quickly understand the importance of our mission. When we launched our first webpage, I sat back and waited for the donations to roll in. When I got tired of waiting, I went back to work at the zoo and waited from there. Lesson one, fundraising does not just happen. Fundraising for an organization that has done absolutely nothing is likely to never happen.

This was our Catch-22: we couldn't do anything without money, and we couldn't get money without doing something. Someone had to give based on trust, and that meant it had to be friends. Thanks to all the people I had met through the zoo and the publicity I had received, I had strong contacts I could reach out to. That began the slow process of building a donor base and implementing some inexpensive projects. We started on familiar ground, in Mexico with monarch butterflies and Kenya with the Samburu people whom I had become friends with while leading tours for the zoo. Slowly, piece by piece, a small organization began to emerge. By now, I was fifty-three years old. It had been thirty-seven years since I first put on the uniform of the Zoological Society of San Diego.

As frustrated as I had become at the zoo, ECOLIFE was about doing the right thing for the world, not getting me out of the zoo and away from a self-created family of animals and animal people. I was the director of the Applied Conservation Division. Though poorly funded and with minimal support from senior executives, it was a good job with a retirement plan and health benefits. Eric was going to be the director at ECOLIFE, but it soon became apparent that we did not have the funds to pay him. He had to find work elsewhere while I continued in my "real" job with the zoo and became the de facto unpaid leader of an organization that had maybe $10-20,000 at a time in the bank.

Over the next few years, we handled the donations carefully and parlayed them into work that provided us with simple stories to explain why our mission was important and different. But fundraising was and still is very hard. It took a lot of attention and a lot of communication; Sunni and I gave it both of those things. With no real background in fundraising, other than what I had learned by osmosis at the zoo, we had to get creative. We needed to be where wealthy people went, and we could hardly afford to do that. Sunni had always been a "foodie," and in no time, she had turned me into one as well. We saved our pennies. When we went out, we went to places beyond our financial ability, but we had a plan. In those bars and restaurants, we met many of our first patrons. While still at the zoo, I had raised money for them by lecturing on high-end cruise ships. When I wasn't at the zoo, the handcuffs were off, and I could speak openly and only about ECOLIFE Conservation.

So out to dinner we would go, most often to restaurants we could barely afford. My beautiful bride would always arrive before me and wait for me at the bar. Sunni is one of the warmest and most out-going people you could ever meet. In no time at all, she would have a couple of new friends surrounding her at the bar. Then I would arrive, and soon we would invite people to travel with us, come to dinner at our house, and finally, support our story, our dream, and our work. In time, we started to gain some traction.

In 2008, things started to come unglued at my real job. While ECOLIFE was not getting rich, it was becoming clear there was an overlap between people I knew and the zoo's donor base. Through my boss, I heard there was concern within the executive branch of the zoo that donors were confused about who they were donating to because of my growing association with ECOLIFE Conservation. Ultimately, the day came when the pressure from the development offices at the zoo came to a head. My employer generously gave me three choices: give up ECOLIFE and continue in my job with the zoo; allow the zoo to absorb ECOLIFE and continue running it; or leave the zoo for ECOLIFE Conservation.

There was not a lot to ECOLIFE at this stage, but it was my dream, my child. I had helped birth ECOLIFE and wanted to see it prosper. Honestly, option one was not going to happen. I would not abandon this child. Running ECOLIFE under the zoo's auspices was an intriguing idea. The zoo had an enormous donor base and a lot of clout. If they really believed in something, they could make it happen. And more than that, they could then influence others. Then there was the other reality. When I was given the opportunity to start and run Applied Conservation at the zoo, it was basically ECOLIFE's philosophy under another name, but the zoo could not get behind it. As a department, we were floundering. As for option three, I was unaware of the upcoming financial recession, but even without that, ECOLIFE could not support my salary, let alone anything else. It seemed like there was no easy decision. Thankfully, I was given some time to think about it.

That evening, Sunni and I had dinner with friends we had met some fifteen years earlier. Their son had a passion for the California condor program. Over time, we had become close friends. They lived ninety minutes away and would come to the Wild Animal Park frequently. We would regularly meet for lunch or dinner, but through all those years, we had never visited each other's homes. Their three kids were homeschooled while the dad worked. He had always described his job as "something like a blacksmith." Anyway, I shared my plight and worries as one would with close friends.

The following day, Sunni called to let me know I had received an overnight package from our friends. After work, I opened the envelope and inside was a note. It said, "Don't be afraid." With it was a check made out to ECOLIFE, enough to cover my salary for the next year. The following day, I resigned and stepped into a new and somewhat uncertain future. That couple has had my back and ECOLIFE Conservation's back ever since. An amazing blacksmith.

ECOLIFE owes everything to my time and experience with the zoo, to those who contribute to ECOLIFE so we can continue our work, and to the fact that our work is impactful and measurable.

We have stumbled, learned, regrouped, and fought our way to success. I was neither a fundraiser nor a marketing person, so every day was filled with rich learning experiences. We chose to launch our stove program internationally but close to home. In the mountains of Central Mexico, generations of monarch butterflies have overwintered in ancient oyamel fir forests. These forests are surrounded by indigenous communities, harvesting hundreds of thousands of trees every year for cooking fuel.

We decided we would introduce a locally designed rural stove called a Lorena. We built one hundred of these large mud-and-brick stoves near the Sierra Chincua and El Rosario butterfly reserves. The stoves were beautiful. Each one had a hand-painted tile on it. Against the background of a monarch butterfly, the tile had the words "Me llamo Lorena y soy amiga de las Mariposas." (My name is Lorena, and I am a friend of the butterflies.) We told families how these new stoves would save the butterflies and went happily on our way.

The following year, preparing to build more stoves, we returned to Mexico and went to see how people had liked the stoves from the previous year. Every single stove was gone. These were not the kind of stoves you just tucked into the trash one day. They would require sledgehammers and pry bars to take them apart. We were baffled. We spoke to our friends and decided these hungry, impoverished families were not too worried about butterflies but more worried about their next meal, so we reworked our pitch.

We started fresh and told people they would spend less time collecting and cutting wood or less money buying wood. We explained their homes would be cleaner, and their kids would be safer and healthier. That was the ticket! Our stove builder became a rock star overnight! Everyone was interested now.

We realized two things: the message about the butterflies was falling on deaf ears, and even more embarrassing for us, most of the families we had provided stoves to did not speak Spanish! The tiles were nearly eight dollars each and meant nothing. So now people loved the stoves, and we could reduce costs by not putting a tile on them. Brilliant. Marketing lesson number two: They wanted the tile. It simply did not matter if they could read the words. It was like the swoosh on a Nike shoe—no one knows what it means, but everyone wants one!

Today, ECOLIFE builds thousands of safe, fuel-efficient stoves in rural communities from Mexico to Kenya and Uganda. We are not the only organization building stoves, but we are one of the very few that balance the quality of the stove against the health needs of the human community and the needs of the environment. Importantly, we select stoves considered culturally appropriate—they need to cook in traditional ways and keep traditional flavors. Most organizations distribute stoves that are fuel-efficient and great for conservation, but that is where the value ends. We see our carefully selected stoves as a holistic solution to many problems, and to do that, they must meet five standards.

First, any stove provided or built by ECOLIFE must be permanent in its placement. We attach a mapped GPS location to every stove and visit it year after year for data collection or maintenance. Our stove work is regularly reviewed and confirmed by a third party. Second, they must have a chimney to remove smoke from their homes. Third, solid construction must allow for cool sides and a stable location for pots of boiling water, stew, or porridge, making them much safer for children.

This little girl (left) was permanently disfigured by burns from an indoor cooking fire. Amon (right) will carry his mother's handprint on his belly forever.

Fourth, they must serve a conservation purpose, so they reduce fuel consumption and, therefore, emissions by at least 50%. Finally, number five, they must be culturally appropriate. They have to cook what the people want, the way they want it cooked.

Stoves are a low-tech solution to a big problem, but we suspected that agriculture would not be so simple. We were right. We have tackled agriculture locally by refining the two-thousand-year-old science of aquaponics, the farming of fish and vegetables in a closed system. This is a fascinating way of growing food developed almost simultaneously by the Aztecs in the New World and the Thai in Asia. The Aztecs built rafts and floated their gardens on lakes rich with fish. The Thai learned that by introducing fish into the rice paddies, the rice grew better, and at harvest time, there were fish to eat with your rice.

While modern systems can be quite complicated, the science itself is simple. Fish rid themselves of nitrogen waste as ammonia. If you have a fish tank at home, you know you need to change out a portion of the water regularly. This removes the ammonia and prevents the fish from dying in their own waste. In aquaponics, the ammonia-laden water goes through biological filters with two different naturally occurring bacteria that break the ammonia down into nitrates. These nitrates are plant food. That water is sent to the plants, which absorb the fertilizer. Now the water is clean and ready to be sent back to the fish. The real beauty of a system like this is that fish can be farmed on only 1% of the water used in traditional fish farms, and there is no runoff or wastewater to spread disease or pollute nearby streams and ponds. Vegetables in these systems are grown in 10% of the space using only 10% of the water and, in general, reach harvest in two-thirds the time. We can literally stack our protein and vegetable farming in a very efficient manner, producing more food in less space and in less time with fewer resources.

For established farmers, change can be difficult, so we choose to also reach out to tomorrow's farmers. By designing a system that fits on a fish tank and creating a dynamic curriculum, we have been able to bring a new vision for sustainable farming to thousands of classrooms across the US. Soon we plan to have full-scale systems packed into shipping containers ready for delivery to the parts of the world that need them the most.

A little boy named Emilien changed my views on many things. Today, tens of thousands of people live healthier lives thanks to stoves that meet environmental *and* human needs. Students in all fifty states have access to a sustainable agriculture curriculum, and we are preparing to launch our first international farm in Uganda. Deep in the history and culture of ECOLIFE are the hard-earned lessons from the zoo and the people I encountered in my work around the world. Most importantly, part of our corporate culture is the commitment that we will *never walk away again.*

The SEARCH *for* EMILIEN

"Well, it's not easy to find something that
you do not know exists."
~*PATRICIA NEDELEA*

I n early 2016, a full sixteen years after the storm in Madagascar,
ECOLIFE's special friend told me it was time to return to
Madagascar. The same friends who, years before, had told me "Don't
be afraid" now scared me to death. Quickly, a couple of other significant donors chimed in. The message was clear: it was time to return

to Madagascar and bring our story full circle, no matter the outcome. Sunni and I were not ready for that. I was told we would have all the funds we needed, and I should plan on being there for as long as it took to come out of the forest with an answer. My heart got well ahead of my brain. I blurted out a yes and thank you without really considering everything that answer would entail. It was going to be very complicated, both practically and emotionally.

In practical terms, it took a lot of planning and coordination to conduct a successful bush trip. Madagascar was notorious for its lack of reliable infrastructure. During the '90s, the project I worked on had offices, trucks, and even networks of people in the forest, but that was then. Things were different now. On top of that, we had mourned. It had been unbelievably hard but starting ECOLIFE Conservation had been a healing salve and protective bandage—a sticky bandage that Sunni and I were about to tear off once again, exposing some very deep wounds.

We started by trying to locate people we had worked with through Project Masoala in Madagascar. One was now a professor at UC Berkeley, and another was posted in London. After so many years, there was no one with the time or connections to help solve my planning issues in Madagascar. It occurred to me that Tiana, my translator, might be the key I needed to unlock the door. Tiana's full name is Heritiana Norolalaina Raharitsimba. I am embarrassed to admit that years ago, her name seemed like alphabet soup to me. It was complicated and unfamiliar, and it had taken a while for me to get used to Tiana, much less all the rest of it. Sixteen years later, I simply did not know her name. This lack of a full name was going to make it hard to find her. All the people I reached out to remembered Tiana, but none knew how to reach her.

In frustration, I googled all the words I could think of related to Tiana, Madagascar, and conservation. I quickly learned Tiana was a far more common name in Madagascar than I had suspected. I also learned I would get nowhere by trying to read each google reference to a Tiana in an attempt to figure out if it was her. I began to search images instead of text pages. Page after page, I could not find anyone resembling Tiana, no matter what I did to refine the search. In fact, I finally realized refining the search only reduced my odds of finding her, so I opened it up and kept staring at photos. Then, late one afternoon, I found a tiny, grainy thumbnail that was definitely Tiana. She was wearing a ball cap with the initials WCS on it. The Wildlife Conservation Society had been a lead participant in Project Masoala.

Feeling some sort of success close at hand, I clicked the link and waited, only to be disappointed. The link was dead, no longer in use, but I could see that it had been a link to a page on a Disney website. Disney was a huge company, and for many, that link to Disney would be of dubious value, but one of the benefits of many years in the field was a solid and diverse connection of friends. I contacted Dr. Jackie Ogden. She and I had worked together at the San Diego Zoo. Devilishly bright and committed, Jackie was snapped up quickly by the conservation world and had gone on to become the Walt Disney Parks and Resorts Vice President of Animals, Science, and Environment. I emailed Jackie, looking for help, and got a prompt reply. Tiana had applied for a grant from Disney, and knowing my story, Jackie was happy to forward Tiana's email address to me. Tiana replied promptly. With that connection in place, I could start to plan a trip.

Our donors were prepared to be generous. Upgraded international flights, funds for charter flights wherever necessary. Money for guides, translators, and vehicles with only a couple of restrictions. First, it was understood we were going to Madagascar and would stay there until we knew what had happened to Antanambao, no matter how long that took. Second, and I pushed back on this, we were to bring along a small film crew to document the journey. That meant more planning. I whined, "We do not know how this is going to end, and I am not sure we need it on film." The reply was simply that no matter how it ended, it was part of our personal history and, more importantly, would be part of ECOLIFE Conservation's history. So my friend Tom Hanscom was chosen to come along as producer, and Josh McMurtrie would be with the cameras and a drone. Sheila Van Metre and Sunni would assist with their cameras and whatever else might be needed.

We had stayed in touch with George's widow and her son Matthew over the years. Our sweet friends had insisted on helping with Matthew's education. They provided funds, but Matthew had to do the work, and he did. As we made our return to Madagascar, Matthew was at the University of California in San Diego, finishing a degree in anthropology. Sadly and frustratingly, Magali could not help us with the search. After the storm and George's death, she had never returned to the Masoala, but she was well connected in Antananarivo and could help. She made arrangements for us at a friend's hotel in Ivato—a nice place close to the airport, as we hoped we would not be spending much time in town.

Only one year earlier, I'd had open-heart surgery to address an aneurysm of my ascending aorta. I seemed to have recovered, but in the months after my surgery, I would occasionally experience chest pains that would drop me to my knees and cause me to vomit from the pain. Several visits to the cardiologist revealed nothing. One day, only weeks before our departure for Madagascar, I found myself in the hospital emergency room after a particularly painful attack. The only thing they could come up with was that it might be my gallbladder and decided to remove it. I asked that we work as quickly as possible to avoid postponing the long-planned trip back to Madagascar. Sunni, along with our donors, was skeptical. The surgery itself would not be a huge deal, but we weren't even sure if it was the cause of my trouble. We decided to proceed, and I reluctantly agreed that if the doctor said I should not go, then I would concede. But Sunni and our friends had to give a little and agree that if the doctor said it was okay, then we would go. In the end, the doctor said I could go, but as best as I could tell, I was the only one happy about the decision.

Sunni gritted her teeth and was pretty unhappy with me for the first few days. After some travel and vigorous hiking, it was clear I was indeed healthy again. Her face brightened, and our search was on.

The plan had been that once I was in Madagascar, Tiana and I would meet and plan the final journey. Like so many things in Madagascar, things changed. Tiana could not get time away to serve as our guide or translator, but she connected me with someone who could contact Jean Luc, the Project Masoala representative who had been living in Antanambao during our previous visits. He could at least serve as our guide to get us to where Antanambao once stood. While I had not heard Jean Luc's name in years, he and Marie Ange had been one of the biggest highlights of our time in Madagascar. We were happy and anxious to see him. As luck would have it, Jean Luc would not be able to meet us in Antalaha for at least a week, which gave us some much-needed planning time. We had some decisions to make.

Unable to go directly to the Masoala, our short-term priority became building our own endurance and filming some of the iconic images associated with this amazing place. Our first stop was the Tsingy de Bemaraha National Park.

We boarded a small, chartered flight to get us close enough to the park that only a short, bumpy car ride was necessary to get us to some reasonable accommodations. I had often flown over Madagascar and witnessed firsthand the complete and utter devastation of the landscape illustrated in many articles about Madagascar, but I was not ready for this. Barren landscape was all there was—dry, barren soils occasionally bisected by streams running red with the soil's blood. This was all there was for more than two hours until we began to fly over the Tsingy de Bemaraha National Park, the only forest in the area that they could not destroy. It stands pristine not because it is a national park, but because it is a forest of stone.

We settled in, arranged for a guide to pick us up in the morning, and began preparing ourselves for a little exercise. We fueled up, got our gear ready, and settled in to rest since we had an early departure. Our guide picked us up in his rickety road-worn car and drove us to the park entrance. We honestly didn't know what to expect and were mildly surprised when we parked and were outfitted with a safety harness. For most of us, this did not bode well. For me, it was worse than I could have predicted. I do not like heights, and I suffer from claustrophobia. As soon as we arrived at the edge of the stone forest, we dove into a cave.

I am not sure why, but I have always had trouble with small spaces and a deep fear of being trapped. As a child, putting my head under the blankets on my bed was an impossibility—I immediately felt as though I could not breathe. Being in nature was the opposite of this terrible fear, until this moment. This cave would be our initial pathway into the stone forest. To enter a cave, I had to be sure I had direct access to a way out, ideally one I could see. It would be folly

One of the ways in to this magnificent stone forest was through an underground passage and added to the drama of our visit.

to put someone between me and the way out, so it made sense to me that I should lead. Our guide quickly nixed that idea because the cave had many twists and turns and a lot of dead ends. Though I had definitely known people to lead when they didn't know where they were going, I was not prepared to be one of them. Instead, I would have to be at the end of the line, so at least I knew there was no one behind me to block my way out. Sweaty and with my stomach in knots, I entered. There was a generous entrance, but things quickly narrowed until I had to remove my day pack and go sideways to squeeze my way through. When it got to where I had to be on my hands and knees, pushing my pack ahead of me, I feared it would be too much. Just when full panic began to set in, there was daylight straight ahead. I scrambled full tilt through the rocks and dust and burst into the light and fresh air. I was momentarily overwhelmed with relief until I realized I was now in a hole with very steep walls. Now for my second fear, it was either three hundred feet straight up or back through the cave like a sniveling child.

The safety harnesses were nice and somewhat comforting until Sunni helpfully noted that she was sure we were only wearing them to make it easier to drag our dead bodies out of the chasm. Once we climbed out of the hole, we were treated to a magnificent vista. There was stone forest for nearly as far as we could see. The sounds of birds and insects filled the air. It became clear that this rugged landscape provided a rich haven for lemurs, birds, reptiles, and insects. After the flight over tragic landscapes, this rich moment filled our hearts.

We had gone through a cave then up a sheer cliff, had enjoyed the view, and were now ready to go. We all looked to the guide with the *which way* look in our eyes. He gathered us together and announced that this would be the hard part. Seriously? He led us around a huge boulder, and there, laid out in front of us, was a very simple (and definitely not OSHA approved) cable bridge spanning a huge canyon filled with sharp shards of jagged rock. To be fair, most of the boards were in place, but the bridge's overall design and

Sunni was caring of my claustrophobia in the cave, but I was caught off-guard by her fear of this bridge. Fortunately, we still laugh about it.

construction were questionable. We were told only one person at a time. I drew the short straw to be the first one across. Only the thought of a cold beer gave me the strength to step onto the bridge and creep my way across.

Sunni would be second, and it was my job to film her as she came across. She had no trouble with the cave and appeared to enjoy the climb, but crossing this rickety bridge was going to be a huge problem. She latched her harness to the cables and white-knuckled the cables on either side of her. She crept slowly with her eyes locked on her feet and her face frozen in a look of sheer terror. Naturally, I wanted her to look good for the camera, so I gently encouraged her to smile and got no reaction. Again, I prodded her with no positive results. I then made a tactical error of suggesting it for a third time. It is important to note that sounds echo in the rocks and canyons. I think even today if you listen closely, you will hear *f%$# you!* echoing through the coldly indifferent spires of rock.

And so this part of the journey went. We moved on to Morandava to see the giant baobab trees. With that done, the moment of truth had arrived. It was time to head for the forest of the Masoala and begin our search in earnest.

While working on the Masoala during the 1990s, the airport in Antalaha had been a relatively busy commercial airport with theoretically regular flights by Air Madagascar. These flights were probably due in large part to the thriving vanilla business—a complicated one that included businessmen, smugglers, and black markets. The airport was badly damaged by cyclone Hudah and was never really repaired. It was cleaned up and made serviceable for a short time after the storm, but its condition deteriorated over time, and eventually, it was closed to commercial traffic. As we circled in, we could see chunks of concrete on the runway. Upon landing, we could see that the terminal was coming apart—windows broken, doors hanging open, and debris everywhere. It was stunning that sixteen years after the storm, its impacts were still spreading. Everything in the region was worse than it had been. It seemed to be a decline with no end in sight.

Before we had unloaded our gear, I was embraced by Jean Luc. Like all of us, he was sixteen years older, but life in Madagascar was hard. This man who had been devilishly handsome now had tired eyes and broken teeth. Later, we learned that he and Marie Ange had broken up, as we understand it, because they were unable to have a child. I remember the look I had gotten when we told people in the village Sunni and I had not had kids. I am sure it was a heavy weight for Jean Luc. We wanted to see Marie Ange, but unfortunately, the time was important. Our arrangements had been made, and we would not even spend a night in Antalaha. We would be on our way in moments, but first, we needed our translator.

Into our life stepped another special person, Ertice Iarozafy, our translator. He was lightly built, young, and had a big perpetual smile and eyes that twinkled with a hint of mischievous joy. He is from Antalaha, speaks English, and is working hard on Spanish. His life is typical of the region. His mother, unfortunately, suffers from leprosy and lives in a nearby leper colony. Ertice works hard at making a living raising chickens and ducks and working in a variety of jobs

Ertice was our translator and, by the end of our journey, a friend for life. His engaging smile and fascination with the world and languages was contagious.

where his language skills could open doors. He is about the same age we imagined Emilien might be and not too dissimilar in appearance. From the beginning, we knew he was going to grow on us.

It was rapidly clear that environmentally, the peninsula had been badly damaged by the cyclone, but worse than that, illegal timber harvesters and rural farmers had taken advantage of the chaos. Now the forest along the coastal areas was largely gone or merely a ghost of its original richness. This had been a storm the peninsula could never fully recover from. Our contacts informed us that two Toyota trucks were ready for us, and we would be able to drive all the way to Cap Est, where George and Magali's remote hotel had been. Though this was good news because it would make our journey somewhat more pleasant, it was also tragic to see the destruction that now allowed us to make this a drive instead of a hike. I could remember walking this pathway, knowing the ocean was one hundred yards away but never being able to see it. That was no longer the case—the ocean was always in plain and barren view.

Rivers were as frequent as I remembered. Smaller ones had rickety bridges, but when we got to wider rivers, we rafted our trucks across on makeshift barges that the Malagasy boatmen maneuvered with remarkable skill. The slow-moving river would edge the rafts downstream, and the men poling the rafts timed our speed perfectly to arrive exactly where we needed to without fighting the forces of nature.

It had become simpler to travel on the Masoala since the storm,
but bridges remained a transient phenomenon.

It was a very full day of travel. We were all in the back of the two trucks, trying to get comfortable on top of our gear, as we pitched from one pothole to another. We were not so much using the trucks for speed as for pack horses. In fact, most of the time, pedestrians and bicyclists would pass by us as we struggled through the difficult terrain. Jean Luc and Ertice regularly told people what we were doing and who we were looking for. No one had answers for us, but we knew that news of our search would radiate and travel ahead of us. By the time we arrived at Cap Est, we were tired, cranky, and sore. Nothing was recognizable at Cap Est. Where there had been romantic palm-thatched bungalows, there was now a simple but sprawling kelp harvesting operation. Where once we had enjoyed eating fresh uni on the beach, there were now scattered carcasses of sea urchins, most likely victims of the "sustainable" kelp harvesting operation.

As tragic as it all was, we were now within a one-day journey to where the little village of Antanambao had stood and the true beginning of our search for lost friends. Dinner was eaten in near silence, each of us deep in our own thoughts. For me, I was considering what we might find and how we might react to the combination of emotions sure to bubble to the surface. The generators were running, and we set about making sure that every battery we had was charged to capacity, then slipped into our primitive accommodations. Spiders and bugs were everywhere, so we set up our tent on the bed, essential gear laid out for an early morning departure. Sunni and I fell easily into our old custom of sleeping in our own tents.

We set off early the next morning for a short ride in the trucks. Once we had gone as far as we could go, we shouldered our packs and began a short but very hot trek to the Iagnobe River. I knew this river well, and seeing it again filled me with amazing memories of Antanambao. Emilien and I had splashed and played in this river. He could swim like a porpoise and would spend hours in the warm brown water. His sister and her girlfriends, muddy from head to toe, would catch tiny fish and insect larvae in tightly woven baskets. At the evening meal, we would find their bounty sprinkled over our bowls of rice. Central to so many memories was an ancient lychee tree near the center of the village. Rich memories of knocking clusters of fruit out with a stick came roaring back. We would sit under that tree and peel and eat the spiny succulent fruit until our fingers were raw from peeling them. At the foundation of all those memories was a deep fear. We knew that no matter what lay ahead, we were only hours from being able to ask about our friends in an area where there might be an answer. Whatever that answer was, we were going to have to be prepared for it—and finally know the end to this story.

We had few connections to set up our expedition, but those we had made—Tiana, Ertice, Jean Luc—had all done their jobs and a ton more. There, on the muddy banks, were the pirogues ready to take us upriver. In my humble opinion, traveling in a pirogue is worse than simply floating down the river on a log. I love kayaking and have often sailed small sailboats, but everything about a pirogue is counterintuitive to me. I was never sure which way to lean or how to help the person poling the pirogue keep it stable. My solution was to tightly grip the sides and turn to stone. I figured that way I was just another piece of cargo.

Tom, Sheila, and Josh left well ahead of us, wanting to be upstream of Sunni, Jean Luc, and me so they could film our arrival. After they were long out of sight, Sunni and I indicated we were ready to go and climbed into the pirogue. Soon the scenery became familiar, and we knew we were drawing close to where Antanambao should be. It was only a few minutes later that we knew there was no Antanambao. It was gone. The little homes that used to be along the river were all gone. Having told so many people we were coming, I had fantasized about a group of old friends meeting us on the beach near the river, but now it became profoundly clear that would not happen. The big cracks in our hearts started to open and bleed again.

We could hear Josh's drone whining overhead. Ahead of us was our little film crew, Ertice, the pirogue pilots, and two or three others at most. It was not what we expected or hoped for. The giant lychee tree I remembered so well was gone—just a big space in the sky where it had stood majestically for decades. We glided up, and the bow of the boat gently slid into the sand. Our team started pulling gear from our boat before Sunni and I could get out, causing the boat to tip. To avoid dunking us into the river, I grabbed the nearest hand and leapt from the boat. I gathered my footing and looked up to say *misaotra*, thank you. It took a moment, and then

I knew I was looking at Emilien and, behind him, smiling from ear to ear, his dad.

Sunni knew instantly it was Emilien, but I had needed a minute for the chubby, round face I remembered to morph gently into the handsome young man helping me from the pirogue. They did know we were coming, which was why only Emilien and his dad were there, our official greeting party. Back in the village, nearly all our old friends were there to greet us, embrace us, and promise to never let us go.

We were quickly introduced to the new Antanambao, just a short ten-minute hike from the Antanambao branded into our memories. The population had changed over the last sixteen years. Babies were born, people moved in, and people moved out, but now our tiny community of two hundred people was four hundred people. And on this day, just a few more because many people who moved away had walked long distances to be there for our return. They came to help cook, say hello, visit, and party endlessly because we were finally home.

Upon our arrival, people vacated their little homes and moved us in. Over the last twenty years, our relationship had evolved from feared strangers to dear friends. As they welcomed us into their homes, we knew we had made the next step. From strangers to friends and, on this visit, from friends to family.

Sadly, there were a handful of friends missing, mostly babies who were tiny at the time of the storm and older people, but our core team was now present and accounted for. Little Julia, the photogenic child we found sick and covered with sores after the storm, was now a beautiful young woman. Emilien's sister had moved to another community but had made a day-long trip to stay in Antanambao and help cook for us.

Emilien has a beautiful girlfriend and a baby that was just eighteen months old during our visit.

For sixteen years, I told the story of tragedy and loss in Madagascar. I was fortunate to have Sunni by my side, always correcting me if

I exaggerated or got something wrong. Now that we were back, I had questions and one that nagged at me the most. In those last moments in the village in 1999, had I understood them correctly? Had they really tried to give us their son? Today, Emilien's mom did

The reunion was emotional, and thanks to phones, internet, and Emilien's willingness to walk miles to see Ertice, we are able to stay in touch.

not look so worried, but her face darkened as she remembered that early morning. There had been a huge discussion between her and her husband. He had felt it was important for Emilien to take any opportunity. His mom looked at me and said, "I was sad because I thought he was too young." She paused for a long moment, then she smiled and said, "He is not too young anymore."

We traveled to Madagascar to bring closure to an important story, but instead of ending a story, it seems a new one is being written. We started ECOLIFE largely because of some of the lessons I learned in Madagascar and because of the special relationship with Emilien, but we had not started ECOLIFE for Emilien or his community. Since founding ECOLIFE, this was our first trip back to Madagascar, and it served as a reaffirmation of our mission. If there is any place in the world that needs safe, fuel-efficient stoves, it is Madagascar. If there is any place that would benefit from sustainable agriculture, it is Madagascar.

We are growing and will continue to grow, and one day soon, Emilien will have the opportunity to work with us to improve his own community. For Sunni and me, it will be the realization of a personal dream to leave Emilien and our world in a better place. For Antanambao, it will be a new beginning laced with hope for a healthier, more prosperous future through sustainable living. We will never walk away again.

Why ECOLIFE CONSERVATION?

After forty-five years in the conservation business, I have come to believe that the word conservation is one of the most misunderstood and misused words in our vocabulary. When we talk about wildlife or resource conservation, we must realize it is a dynamic process. You cannot pick and choose components of a system to conserve any more than you can choose to protect your liver and ignore your heart. Conservation demands and deserves no less than a holistic approach.

So many of us in this field have fought with laser-like focus for a species, as I did for the California condor or others have done for any one of hundreds of other species of interest. But for all those efforts, the ecosystems that support those species and hundreds of thousands of others continue to decline. Without healthy ecosystems, a home for these animals and plants to survive in, single species recovery programs accomplish next to nothing in terms of real conservation.

Years ago, conservation groups began to talk about "community-based" conservation, which created work for people as guides and guards. This was the first effort to add people to the equation. Over the years, the reality settled in. Relative to community size, there were very few jobs. In the case of guards, they often guarded a resource their friends and families depended on for survival. This clearly led to conflicts and corruption. Human needs simply could not be met by providing a small select handful of people with a job.

After the storms in Madagascar and the failures of other programs I had watched or participated in, I needed to take a time-out and rethink how to move forward more effectively. I recognized that the leading cause of extinction was habitat loss, which was profoundly driven by agriculture. We are finally recognizing that habitat loss is also tied to climate change, and a significant driver of climate change is agriculture. If we wanted to strike at the core causes of extinction, we needed to look at what we eat, how we produce it, and how we prepare it. Narrowly focused species-by-species or habitat-by-habitat programs were not going to do it. We needed to find a new way, and this was the birth of ECOLIFE Conservation.

- An organization that would redefine "community-based" as something that benefited every person in the community.
- An organization that might use a wildlife flagship like the gorilla or monarch butterfly but whose work would have positive impacts across the entire ecosystem.
- An organization that measurably improved lives and conserved habitats.
- An organization whose work has the potential of global impact.

It has been a long process and not always easy, but now, ECOLIFE is unique among conservation groups because of its attention to these details and its balanced focus on humans and our resources.

The real challenge faced by those wanting to do solid conservation is relying on great data provided by strong fact-driven research without getting lost in the data and evolving into a research team. Many organizations have fallen into this trap over the years. Research can be a pitfall for conservation organizations because it is often easier to do than applying solutions. If research is done well, then there is no wrong answer. The same is not true of implementing conservation that will need to survive the test of even a few years.

ECOLIFE Conservation has adopted sustainable agriculture, initially in the form of aquaponics, as one of two areas of focus. With this one technique, we can reduce the amount of land needed for crop production. Aquaponics can be done on land previously considered non-arable, significantly reduce water use, and produce fish and vegetables. As an example, in 2012, about 120,000 acres were dedicated to lettuce production in the US. With aquaponics, that same crop volume could be produced on 12,000 acres leaving 108,000 acres for solar farming and/or habitat restoration.

The second area of focus was driven by the need to reduce negative health impacts on people and empower them to improve their quality of life. Three-stone fires are still used by more than three billion people in the world, and the environmental impact is enormous. With smoke from indoor cooking fires being the leading cause of preventable deaths, these three-stone fires are an obvious target for ECOLIFE Conservation. For example, each stove built in Mexico has an annual carbon reduction value equal to removing an average car from the road for one year. If every family in the world who needs a stove was provided with one, it would be the equivalent of removing five hundred million cars from the road, or roughly one-third of all automobiles in the world. This allows us to improve the health of families receiving a stove and improve the quality of life for people around the world, all while protecting forest resources.

In 2021, ECOLIFE Conservation's improved cookstove program in Mexico became a Gold Standard certified project because of its broad achievements in reducing carbon outputs, protecting forests, improving community health, and creating fair local employment. This challenging certification process is overseen by the Gold Standard in Geneva, Switzerland, and qualifies ECOLIFE to market Verified Emission Reductions (carbon offsets) generated by the installation of safe, fuel-efficient stoves around the Monarch Butterfly Biosphere Reserve in Mexico. With this achievement, the stove program moves us a step closer to being financially self-sustaining.

Maybe more importantly, Gold Standard certification assures ECOLIFE's donor community that quantifiable steps are being taken that result in verified positive impacts on communities and the environment. As you consider how best to invest your humanitarian and conservation dollars, I hope you will explore ECOLIFE Conservation and become part of our family.

ACKNOWLEDGMENTS

I have spent a lot of time writing this book, but nothing is more difficult than the acknowledgements. There is an incredible fear that I will overlook the gifts of someone amazing and not think of it until the book has gone to press. To all of you on that invisible list, I am sorry, but you have to know that you are loved.

Much to the chagrin of dear friends, I have often done credits at the end of a lecture and forgotten to thank my wife. So while I will list my friends, colleagues, and counselors separately, I need to reserve a special place to thank my wife, Sunni Black. Supportive, collaborative, independent, inspiring, beautiful, elegant, soft, rugged, cautious and daring, she seems to know when to put it out there and when to pull it in. She knows which fork I should use and which wine will go with yet another meal from a kitchen filled with food seemingly made of love. Following her lead and finding support and love in her arms has been everything to me.

One of the biggest motivations in writing this has been being a parent. Emily, David, and their children were an unexpected bonus in my life. I have learned you can never spend enough time with your kids, and I know I have had less time with my children than most loving parents. This book is the story of where I was and what I was doing. I love you for being so forgiving and returning so much love to me. For you, and everyone else's children, please know how hard many people have tried to leave you a better world. Speaking for many of my generation, we apologize for our failures but are optimistic that you have a clear vision as to how to make this planet a healthier and more pleasant place to live and raise your families.

I have been blessed by amazing people throughout my life and always at the right time and the right place. Among those that are no longer here, Howard and Josephine, my mom and dad will forever live in my heart, rarely sure of what I was really up to (or were you?) they were always there with support and encouragement. Professor Konrad Lorenz for being a penpal, Dr. Art Risser for kind leadership, K.C. Lint for his chickens, and Professor Frank Ogasawara who taught me to teach with both passion and compassion.

Veronika Areskoug and Lena Eriksson for enduring unrelenting and needless abuse in Paraguay while staying true to their mission of science and conservation.

Among my friends and mentors are photographers, scientists, teachers, and of course, the wildlife that stole my heart as a child. You have always had a hand at my back saying "don't be afraid". Tom Hanscom could be counted on to make a good idea better and to kill a bad idea before anyone else knew about it. Leading me, supporting me, pushing me, providing photos, or just loving me are Judy Bernstein, Pamela Black, PJ Campbell, Patricia Dintrone, Erin Grey, Eric Hallstein, Dorothy Huhn, Joe Kita, Dave Ledig, Steve and Cathi Shultz, Helen Snyder, Noel Snyder, Linn Splane, Don Sterner, and Roy Toft. And of course, my siblings and their spouses, David and Ivana Toone, Susan and Larry House, Barbara and Jeff Smith.

PHOTOGRAPHY CREDITS

Chapter 1: Centipede, anankkml, Depositphotos.com

Chapter 2: Wyandotte Chicken, cynoclub, Depositphotos.com; Bill with a gopher snake in Poway by Howard Toone

Chapter 3: Pygmy goat NynkevanHolten, Depositphotos.com; Bill with Jim the gorilla, photo by Howard Toone

Chapter 4: Abyssinian ground hornbill at San Diego Zoo, USA by Jerry Thompson is licensed under CC by 2.0, modified from original—deleted background, grayscale

Chapter 5: Vulture, Turkey by Alan Schmierer, public domain, modified from original—deleted background, grayscale

Chapter 6: Pacific-slope flycatcher by Becky Matsubara is licensed under CC by 2.0, modified from original—image reversal, deleted background, grayscale

Chapter 7: California Condor by Jim Bahn is licensed under CC by 2.0, modified from original—deleted background, grayscale

Chapter 8: Condor egg, photo by Sunni Black

Chapter 9: Feather, photo by Sunni Black

Chapter 10: Andean condor, San Diego Zoo Wildlife Alliance; Press photo with Andean condor, San Diego Zoo Wildlife Alliance; Puppets, San Diego Zoo Wildlife Alliance; Noel Snyder, photographer unknown; Condor egg in nest, photo by Noel Snyder; Redrock egg pickup, photographer unknown

Chapter 11: California condor chick, San Diego Zoo, Ron Garrison, public domain, modified from original—image reversal, deleted background, grayscale; CBS News March 31, '83; Chumash elders, photographer unknown

Chapter 12: Young giraffe by Kitty Terwolbeck is licensed under CC by 2.0, modified from original—deleted background, grayscale; Dying condor, San Diego Zoo Wildlife Alliance; Johnny Carson, photo by *The Tonight Show*

Chapter 13: Male peregrine falcon, by Roy W Lowe, is licensed under CC by 2.0, modified from original—image reversal, deleted background, grayscale; Letter from USFWS, from the author's archive

Chapter 14: Monach butterfly, thawats, DepositPhotos.com

Chapter 15: Monarch chrysalis, sirichai2514, Depositphotos.com; Flying monarchs, photo by Sunni Black; Sunni in butterflies, photo by Bill Toone

Chapter 16: Monarch Butterflies, by Bernard Spragg, public domain, modified from original—image reversal, deleted background, grayscale; Firewood on horse, photo by Roy Toft; Dead butterflies, photo by Tom Hanscom

Chapter 17: Paraguay, systemm, Depositphotos.com; Bill with Anteater, photo by Veronika Areskoug and Lena Eriksson

Chapter 18: Lemur, Margo1956, Depositphotos.com; Skull, photo by Bill Toone; Masoala trek, photo by Roy Toft

Chapter 19: Blue coua (Coua caerulea), by Olaf Oliviero Riemer, is licensed under CC by 3.0, modified from original—image reversal, deleted background, grayscale; Bill and Emilien, photo by Sunni Black

Chapter 20: Tropical lychee, Kovaleva_Ka, Depositphotos.com; Emilien ready to travel, photo by Sunni Black

Chapter 21: Melanempis scoliiformis, Bottle green Madagascan cuckoo, by OUSGS Bee Inventory and Monitoring Lab is licensed under CC by 2.0, modified from original—image reversal, deleted background, grayscale

Chapter 22: African elephant, fouroaks, Depositphotos.com; Horse plowing in Michoacán, photo by Roy Toft

Chapter 23: ECOLIFE butterfly logo; Little girl with burns, photo by Bill Toone; Amon with burns, photo by Alexis Chavez

Epilogue: Young chameleon, Eric Isselée, AdobeStock.com; Cave in the Grand Tsingy, photo by Sunni Black; Bridge out of Grand Tsingy, photo by Bill Toone; Ertice Iarozafy, photo by Sunni Black; River crossing, photo by Josh McMurtrie; Emilien and Bill, photo by Sunni Black